D0455198

# A Heart
# Like His

# A HEART LIKE HIS

MAKING SPACE FOR
GOD'S LOVE IN YOUR LIFE

VIRGINIA H. PEARCE

DESERET
BOOK

SALT LAKE CITY, UTAH

In some cases, the circumstances and names of individuals described in the text have been changed.

© 2006 Virginia H. Pearce

All rights reserved. No part of this book may be reproduced in any form or by any means without permission in writing from the publisher, Deseret Book Company, P. O. Box 30178, Salt Lake City, Utah 84130. This work is not an official publication of The Church of Jesus Christ of Latter-day Saints. The views expressed herein are the responsibility of the author and do not necessarily represent the position of the Church or of Deseret Book Company.

DESERET BOOK is a registered trademark of Deseret Book Company.

Visit us at deseretbook.com

Library of Congress Cataloging-in-Publication Data

Pearce, Virginia H.
  A heart like His : making space for God's love in your life / Virgina H. Pearce.
    p.  cm.
  Includes bibliographical references.
  ISBN 1-59038-544-6 (hardbound : alk. paper)
  1. Mormon women—Religious life. 2. God—Love. I. Title.
  BX8641.P38 2006
  248.4'89332—dc22           2005027122

Printed in the United States of America        18961
R. R. Donnelley and Sons

10   9   8   7   6   5   4   3

To Jim and Rosemary, Richard, Laura, Blair, Emily, Dave,

Heidi, Randy, Amy, John, James, and Anna,

who graciously ignore my shortcomings

and love me, no matter what

# CONTENTS

———— ❦ ————

# CONTENTS

# ACKNOWLEDGMENTS

It is impossible to acknowledge everyone who has helped bring to print this particular book. Because the topic is so personal in nature, the writing has been influenced by every person who has extended the gift of charity to me over a lifetime, beginning with my parents and including all of the extraordinary human beings it has been my unearned privilege to know. However, the ideas that started our Relief Society committee on this exciting journey of discovery were generously offered by Cyril I. A. Figuerres. He and his wife, Aileen, powerfully teach by precept and example the joy of extending God's love to others. I wish to acknowledge also all those who took the challenge to experiment with a more open heart— both the women of Relief Society and our priesthood leaders. I hesitate to name all who contributed for fear of leaving someone out but must give particular thanks to members of the presidency: Shannon Christiansen, Mary Mabey, Jan Lambert, and Mary Lou Holman; as well as my walking friends: Dixie, Bonnie, and Joan. Their enthusiasm, goodness, and love continue to nourish me.

The folks at Deseret Book have been cheerleaders *extraordinaire*. In particular, Jana Erickson, Cathy Chamberlain, Emily Watts, and Richard Peterson have offered consistent encouragement and their much-needed editorial eyes. Thank you also to designer Sheryl Smith, who so carefully developed the graphics in ways that complement the book's message, and to typesetters Tonya Facemyer and Laurie Cook, for their skillful work.

I am indebted as well to Phyllis Barber, Karen Carlson, Laurel Olsen, Joan Reynolds, and my children, who read all or parts of the manuscript, giving specific help as well as encouragement. The book is infinitely better because of them.

And a final acknowledgment of women everywhere, but especially the covenant women of Relief Society. Their individual goodness inspires me, their love supports me, and their eagerness to change and become more like the Savior gives me energy to move forward.

# INTRODUCTION

———— ❧ ————

The love of God truly is the most joyous and delicious thing we can experience on this earth. It is so good that when we are filled with it, we are consumed with a desire that others should feel it too.

But experiencing the love of God can be an elusive thing. Though we believe that His love is constant and unchanging, we seem unable as mortals to consistently feel it. And if we can't feel it, we are unable to help others feel it.

This book is meant to help the reader explore and experiment with the simple concept of opening her heart—simply making space for the Lord and others. Because this experiment is more about *becoming* than *doing*, it is simple, doesn't consume time, actually creates energy, and is therefore self-perpetuating.

Although the suggestions are modest and quite easy to implement, the outcomes could not be more profound, for we are, after all, in search of a new heart—a heart like His.

*Chapter One*

# "SPLITTING THE SKY IN TWO"

———— ❧ ————

*The world stands out on either side*
*No wider than the heart is wide;*
*Above the world is stretched the sky,—*
*No higher than the soul is high.*
*The heart can push the sea and land*
*Farther away*
*On either hand;*
*The soul can split the sky in two,*
*And let the face of God shine through.*
*But East and West will pinch the heart*
*That can not keep them pushed apart;*
*And he whose soul is flat—the sky*
*Will cave in on him by and by.*

EDNA ST. VINCENT MILLAY *"Renascence"* [1912] last lines

I guess I could start," Ellen said, leaning forward in the rocking chair to take a 3x5 card from her purse on the floor. Seven other women immediately relaxed. We were gathered in a circle, members of a stake Relief Society committee that had accepted an assignment the month before and had now come together to report. We'd had the opening prayer, restated the assignment, and now the floor was open for discussion. Each of us hesitated, our thoughts flying, but our tongues uncharacteristically still, until Ellen, the quietest of all, came to our rescue.

"Well, I baked some cinnamon rolls, and then I just tried to think of someone who wouldn't expect a visit from me." She giggled self-consciously and rubbed the thumb of her right hand back and forth on the wooden arm of the rocker as she tentatively continued. "I was just about sick I was so nervous, but it helped to think about people up and down the street and then about my heart." Ellen concentrated on the card in her hand. It was filled with small, perfectly penciled notes. "I kept thinking about making my heart soft and enlarged and available—like we talked about last month. Maybe that's why I thought of making cinnamon rolls—you know, a warm, squishy heart?"

The other seven of us rippled an encouraging response to

her humor, and Pauline fairly beamed approval at Ellen from across the living room.

*She's darling, but that's not exactly fair,* I thought from my chair on the other side of the fireplace. We weren't supposed to *do* anything special, like bake rolls or make extra visits. I didn't say anything, though, because I didn't want the floor, and more than that I was mesmerized by the quiet charm of Ellen's voice as she became more and more animated.

When my friend recommended that I invite Ellen to serve on this Relief Society committee, she had described Ellen as "understated." I answered that there were plenty of overstated people in the world and that I would welcome an understated model. So I was more than a bit surprised that Ellen would have the confidence to lead out the way she was doing that night. Understated, yes, but lacking confidence? Maybe not.

Ellen continued, "I took some rolls to the Vincents and then went to see a couple of quiet, elderly ladies who don't get out to church. They were surprised to see me." Ellen actually twinkled, as if she had pulled off a shoemaker-and-the-elves stunt. "And then I went to see Mina, a friend from Eastern Europe. I don't keep in touch with her as much as I should." Ellen finally stopped rubbing the satiny wood with her thumb, and she placed the card in her lap. Then, lacing the fingers of both hands together, she leaned forward and drew us into the story of a woman coming to a foreign land with three small children and a handsome husband. But within a short time their world of opportunity was suddenly shattered by her husband's early death.

Ellen said, "I'm sure that nothing was ever the same again for Mina. But she's overcome so much. When you think that she learned a new language, managed to make a living with very little education or training, learned to drive, and did all that it takes to rear children, it's unbelievable. But, you can imagine that everything's been hard for her. You just feel it. Because of the language, she often misunderstands people's motives and imagines ill will. Even with that, she's friendly and willing to make herself part of things. The children are all adults now and doing well, but I sometimes wonder if you ever lose the feeling of being isolated when you grow old in a foreign country. But how would I know!"

Ellen's hands went back on the arms of the rocker as she sat up straight. "Yes, when I was making the cinnamon rolls, I had a feeling that I wanted to take some to her."

Almost startled by her own confidence, Ellen glanced around our circle. "None of you know me very well, but you probably guessed that when I showed up at the stockroom in the preexistence, there must have been a back order on being big and bold, so in this life I'm short and quiet."

Ellen dropped her voice into a confessional tone, "I've always wondered if there really is a spot for short, quiet people. The rest of you always seem to have more fun. But, really, when I was rolling out the dough and thinking about those people, I must admit I was pretty close to having fun. I just put my shoulders back like we talked about, so that my heart could have more room, and I even said out loud: 'I'll just go do it!'" Ellen stopped and looked up, waiting for a response, but no one said anything. Our silence coaxed her on.

"But guess what?" she resumed. "Even though it was scary to knock on the doors, every single person was happy to see me. The best one though was Mina. The weather had been stormy, and she told me that she was sick and had been indoors for days. She couldn't believe that someone had thought about her."

Ellen looked up and past the tops of our heads. For just a moment it was as if we had disappeared and she were alone in the room as the evening darkness began to sneak in through the windows. We held our breath until she started talking again, almost to herself. "I'm so glad it was me," she said quietly. "I don't care about being big and bold anymore. I just want to change my heart, and I think it's starting to happen."

The committee meeting lasted for about two hours that night. Years afterward the eight women gathered wouldn't be able to remember exactly what was said by whom or in what order, but most of us would echo Ellen's feeling: "I wanted to change my heart, and I think it started to happen that night."

The meeting had grown out of a church calling, where I, along with several women, found myself on a Relief Society committee organized to help women in our stake feel the love of the Lord in their lives more deeply and on a more frequent basis. We planned to use our stake women's conference as at least one of the places where we could do this. As members of the committee, we felt that we could move forward in our assignment if we first learned better for ourselves what it means to live more consistently with softened, more open hearts; hearts that are more available to God and to others— souls that were less flat. And so we decided to put all of the other usual tasks, such as designing invitations, making decorations, preparing refreshments, deciding on speakers, and the

> *If I could have one thing happen for every woman in this Church, it would be that they would feel the love of the Lord in their lives daily.*
> Bonnie D. Parkin[1]

6

like, temporarily aside and experiment *personally* with the principles we hoped to teach at the conference.

We knew that when we felt loved by the Lord, we automatically treated other people more lovingly, but we wondered if we could perhaps do more to initiate a change in the condition of our own hearts that would *then* result in our feeling an added measure of love from the Lord and in turn help others feel His love. And the circle could continue. We all wondered, could this be an accurate hypothesis? Could we actually alter the condition of our own hearts in a way that would make it possible to "split the sky in two, and let the face of God shine through"? Why not devise an experiment?

All eight of us were eager to begin but also a bit cautious. We each had busy lives and a history of failed programs and resolves. We were wary of making a list—no matter how small—of more things to do. We wondered, really wondered, if our hypothesis could be verified. Would simply opening our hearts to others also invite Him into our hearts? In the past we felt we had prayed for His love to fill our hearts, *then* we turned toward others with a softened heart. This would be starting at the other end, if you will. We didn't know what would happen, but this was to be an experiment. So we went forward, feeling that we had nothing to lose and perhaps a great deal to learn.

We were experimenting with principles, in the tradition of Alma. As we opened our hearts in love, we wondered if the seeds would in fact swell and begin to enlarge our souls, or if they would just shrivel up and blow away on a breeze.

As a committee, we outlined a plan: to simply be more aware of the condition of our hearts, and with this awareness, crack them open a bit wider. We agreed to do this during encounters that would present themselves in the natural flow of our lives. Then we would honestly report what had occurred. Those were the rules of the experiment—the only rules. The eight of us thought it seemed quite easy, and our expectations were modest. We got out our little planners and agreed on a Thursday evening in May, when we would gather again and report what, if anything, had happened.

As you might expect, the month passed ever so swiftly, and there we were on a warm spring evening in a circle of chairs in my living room, where Ellen was to be the first to describe her experience. We went over the purpose of the experiment: our desire to open our hearts to others in the hopes that they could feel the love of the Lord more fully in their lives. We reiterated the rules of what we were now calling our "Awareness Experiment":

1. To be more aware of the condition of our **hearts** and with that awareness to keep them more **open** toward others.

2. To do this in **the normal course of our lives,** in other words, not put any extra activities into our day—no extra visits, no preparing of casseroles, etc. Above all, **people were not to become "projects,"** and our lives were not to be filled with more things to do!

3. **Notice the Spirit,** and be willing to come together and **honestly report** what happened or hadn't happened.

Well, going back to that evening in May, we gathered. The time for honestly reporting had arrived, and only Ellen was initially prepared to break the silence. Only Ellen with her neatly written 3x5 card felt that she had participated in the experiment, that she had "done it right." The rest of us were mumbling about how fast time had flown.

However, after Ellen finished her report, the rest of us hesitantly began to reach back into our memories of the past weeks for those moments that might have seemed quite small at the time, but as we sat together were beginning to seem more significant.

"I forgot about it until now, but there was this one morning," I recalled, wondering if what I was about to say would sound stupid. "I was doing the usual—long list, telephone, other things, I don't know—and my doorbell rang. It was Ann, a neighbor whom I visit teach. Except for an occasional wave as we come and go in the neighborhood, she's someone I usually see only when I do my monthly visiting. She had stopped by because someone dropped off something for me at her work, knowing that she lived near me and could conveniently return it. I opened the door to take it from her and thank her, and just as I was about to say 'Have a great day!' and wave her on, I thought about our experiment and about my little closed heart.

"Bingo! *Open it up, Virginia!* So, almost instantaneously, I heard myself say, 'Have you got a minute to come in?' This is hard to believe, because I always think that *everyone* else is in a hurry (like me) and that I shouldn't impose. But, much to my surprise, she said, 'Sure,' and came right in. We sat down in the living room and chatted away. We ended up laughing and talking comfortably for a few minutes, and then she went on her way."

As I continued talking, I lost my hesitancy. Yes, this *was* important, not stupid. I stopped, thought of my friend Ann and our conversation, warming to the memory. "Maybe I'm making too much out of this, but I have a feeling that everything is just a little different for the two of us now. We're friends—even, balanced friends. I mean, I called her later that day for a telephone number. I'd never done that before. I'm no longer just *her* visiting teacher who goes to *her* living room. She's been in *my* house. We're regular friends. It's an open-heart thing." I thought back, irritated with myself, and said, "Me and my schedule and thinking that everyone is punching a time clock! I've *got* to be tuned into this schedule thing. It's definitely a red flag for me. It's a warning that my heart is shutting down."

Now I was really on my soapbox and probably talking a little too loudly. "After all," I continued with disgust, "I wasn't fifteen minutes more behind at the end of the day than I would have been otherwise, and I'll bet she wasn't, either. Actually it turned out to be one of the brightest spots of my week!"

I felt, more than heard, the circle of friends congratulating me. Actually, there was a bit of silence as we all looked around for someone else to report.

Barbara hesitated. Reaching for a strand of her straight blond hair, she tucked it behind her ear and said, a little tentatively, "Well, I was out-of-town quite a bit. Does it count if my 'open-heart' conversation was with someone on the plane, not someone in the stake?" We all started to laugh—along with Barbara. Yes, this experiment had grown out of a Relief Society committee, but how absurd that we would think that any good thing we do should be limited to boundary lines, whether they be geographic or religious or otherwise!

We would talk about this a great deal in the coming months as we began to understand more and more that we were experiencing a change in *our own hearts; becoming* differ-ent within ourselves, not *doing* something to someone else. Obviously, if we are *becoming new creatures* we will be consistently practicing—whenever, wherever. If having an open heart is just a matter of doing, we can turn it off and on like a switch—be a good mother, an irritable coworker, a good gospel doctrine teacher, a withholding daughter-in-law, and so on.

Barbara took heart from our laughter and began to describe an experience she had had with a seat-mate on the plane. At first they just exchanged pleasantries, but before Barbara knew it, the woman was talking about the conflict she was feeling—between managing her career and nurturing her family. Barbara said to us, "I instinctively knew that I shouldn't give advice. My only job was just to keep praying and thinking about my heart—is it open,

> *In contrast to the institutions of the world, which teach us to* know *something, the gospel of Jesus Christ challenges us to* become *something. . . . The gospel of Jesus Christ is the plan by which we can become what children of God are supposed to become. . . . Charity is something one becomes.*
>
> Elder Dallin H. Oaks[2]

nonjudgmental, loving, accepting? It was quite easy. I just listened and responded from my heart, and this lovely woman talked and talked.

"By the time we landed, we really cared about each other. She said, 'Thanks for letting me talk. I guess I didn't realize until I went on and on how much I care about my family. They really are more important to me than my job. I know what I'm going to do. Thanks for helping me figure it out.' Wow. Usually I get on a plane feeling grungy because I'm so tired. I'm telling you, I walked off the plane feeling better than if I'd slept all the way!"

No silence this time. We all turned, as if with one head, to the next person. It was Pauline, and she willingly shared something she had done. She told about going to the gym to work out a couple of weeks before.

"As I walked in with my daughters, a woman greeted me enthusiastically—as though she really knew me. 'Hi, Pauline!' Panic. The face didn't look remotely familiar. I couldn't pull up a name or even a context. But, just as I was ready to fake a friendly response and go to the other side of the workout room, I thought of our experiment and paid attention to my heart. It was all shriveled up—moving to the back of my chest—protected, hard, and cold. I quickly talked to myself, *Wait a minute, Pauline! This is your chance to experiment!* So I said, 'I'm sorry. I can't place you. Tell me your name.'"

The door flew open to what Pauline called the most wonderful hour of conversation. "We moved to exercise machines next to each other, and my friend from kindergarten, whom I had not seen since high school, ended up telling me her life story. It had been a tough one. We cried together as she described about what she had gone through, but the real tears came when she told me that she had been rebaptized that very week and was anticipating a new and good life ahead of her.

"My heart at the end of the hour was a different heart. It was the heart we've talked about so much; softened, opened, filled with His love, reaching out, nonjudgmental, positive, kind, affirming.

> ———— 🐝 ————
>
> *Love is a softening of the heart; pride is a hardening.*
> Marilyn Arnold[3]

"After we finished exercising, I introduced her to my girls. It was as if I were introducing a long-lost loved one. And I guess that's really what she is. I know I don't love her like the Lord does, but there really was some of that in there." Then Pauline paused and said more quietly, "I can't believe I almost missed the whole experience because I habitually keep my heart closed up and move on when I don't recognize someone. I guess it's pride. It's such a stupid thing. And guess what? It didn't take any extra time out of my day!" Pauline raised one closed-fisted arm in a triumphal salute. "Life is good!"

And so it went around the circle. Two hours flew by. Everyone had at least one simple story to tell. We had come into the room thinking that we really hadn't done very well, but as we listened to one another and reflected on our moments of awareness, when we had consciously opened our hearts, our enthusiasm literally exploded. Even as we sat together we felt our hearts changing in profound ways. The world around us suddenly seemed new. We began to feel directly His love for us, and we were surprised at how energizing it was to help others feel God's love for them because of the way we thought about them and treated them.

As we tried to describe what we were learning, we began to laugh. This wasn't as revolutionary as we thought. It was pretty basic stuff—Christianity 101, if you please! Why did it seem so effortless and brand new? And it took virtually *no* extra time. Except of course, for Ellen, the understated overachiever, who insisted that making several batches of cinnamon rolls was part of the "natural flow of her life!" Perhaps we had spent a lot of time in our lives going about "doing" good rather than letting the

Lord help us "become" good in our hearts. We loved it and couldn't quit talking about it and our desire to change even more.

This little book, then, becomes an explanation of our committee's journey and a personal invitation from me to you, my reader friend, to join us in opening your heart just a crack wider now and then. Because of our shared experiences, I really am convinced that having an open heart does "split the sky in two and let the face of God shine through." I hope that the simplicity of our experiment won't insult you, that you will think it inviting to consider your own heart. Perhaps my friends and I are the only ones on the planet who were making life harder than it really is, but maybe, just maybe, it's harder for you than it needs to be also!

Think of the women in this chapter and their stories. Were you particularly drawn to any of them? Which one? Why? As you consider opening your own heart, what stumbling blocks might you anticipate?

Find one or more friends who might like to work with you, people with whom you feel comfortable who will want to talk back and forth as you all experiment with, redefine, and add to the concepts in this book.

*Chapter Two*

# WHAT IS AN OPEN HEART?

────────── ❧ ──────────

*And their hearts were open*
*and they did understand.*

3 NEPHI 19:33

The heart is a physical organ. It is also the center of our emotional and spiritual life. Exactly how all the functions are connected no one understands, but there is an undeniable relationship. I cannot attempt to describe it for you, only how it feels for me. At the risk of sounding a little odd, I can tell you than I can actually feel my heart change its physical texture, size, and position, in relation to my spiritual condition. It gets hard and tiny and moves back behind my chest wall when I am angry and withdrawn and self-absorbed. On the other hand, when I am filled with love and reaching out to others, it softens and warms and moves forward—it is enlarged and full. Perhaps my mind is a trifle overactive, but the imagery works very well for me. After all, the scriptures use it—softened and enlarged, or hardened and cold—and so does Dr. Seuss, when he describes the Grinch's heart as growing "three sizes that day."[4]

These physical descriptors are critical for me to keep in mind because they are the signals I have come to rely on to help me know when I need to make a change in my outlook and behavior.

When I was a young girl, I had the immense good fortune to take creative dance from Virginia Tanner, the American pioneer of children's dance. My mother understood Virginia's vision of dance—a belief in the beauty of creative expression. And although I and most of my friends did not become professional dancers, through her love of music and movement, Virginia taught us much about the beauties of life. I particularly loved the end of each class when we would put on our

---

*An Open Heart Is:*

ENLARGED

SOFT

OPEN

WARM

CLOSE TO THE SURFACE OF THE CHEST WALL

---

*An Closed Heart Is:*

SHRIVELED

SMALL

HARD

CLOSED

COLD

TUCKED AWAY DEEP INSIDE A PROTECTIVE WALL

"Ginny Gowns." They came in pastel colors and were made of soft, flowing fabric. And they were full. Yards and yards of cloth that swept along as we ran, leapt, and twirled to the lyrical music from the pianist in the corner of the large room.

These spontaneous dances were not choreographed, and I can still hear Miss Virginia's voice urging us to make our own beautiful patterns. Echoing in my memory is her call to dance with our "magic eye." That meant to open our arms, drop our shoulders, breathe deeply, and lift forward with our bodies.

> *The word is good, for it beginneth to enlarge my soul.*
> ALMA 32:28

I think of my magic eye when I feel I am shriveling inward, crunched up with irritation and harboring a closed, critical, hardened heart. It is a helpful physical image. As I physically drop my shoulders, breathe deeply, and expand my chest, it reminds me to drop my defenses and ask the Lord to open and soften my heart.

Body language not only describes how I feel, it communicates the same to others. If I lean toward someone who is speaking, she feels my attentiveness and interest. Touching someone lightly can convey concern, while dropping my eyes can signal discomfort. If I move slightly away and fold my arms in a closed position in front of my chest I communicate a desire for distance.

I came in from my early morning walk some time ago, invigorated and ready to start my day. But as I turned into my driveway, the beauty of the morning evaporated, and the pressures of the day crowded in on me. Going through the back gate, I opened the kitchen door, and within seconds I had poured Cheerios into a plain white bowl, picked up a spoon, and opened the planner beside me, adding between hurried bites to my to-do list. Characteristically the list was much longer than the day, but I felt energetic and was just about to get on with it all when my husband started down the stairs, scriptures in hand.

"I don't know what happened, but I'm just a few minutes early getting ready for work, and I've run onto the most amazing scripture."

I should have seen that as a wonderful invitation, but, Martha-like, I was "careful and troubled about many things" (Luke 10:41), and inside, this hard-hearted wife responded with an irritable edge. *Well, isn't that nice for you, but I'm already more than a few minutes behind with my day!* I didn't say that, because sometimes I remember how to talk nicely even when I feel otherwise, but I took my husband's invitation as an intrusion.

"Oh, I'm really in a hurry," I responded. "Can we do it tonight?" Mid-stairs, he cheerfully answered, "That's fine. No problem," and he turned around and went back upstairs.

But that is not the end of the story because by that time I was a seasoned experimenter, and it took only the amount of time for him to get back to the bedroom door for me to recognize that I had reacted out of a somewhat shriveled heart. I heard the conversation in my head: irritated, critical, and all about me. So I dropped my shoulders, took a deep breath, and let my heart grow just a little softer before I said, "Wait a minute, I'll get my scriptures and be right up." Remarkably enough,

> *As you increase in innocence and virtue, as you increase in goodness, let your hearts expand, let them be enlarged towards others.*
> JOSEPH SMITH[5]

his heart had not hardened in response during those few intervening moments, and we had the sweetest five minutes, talking about a particular verse.

Experimenting with an open heart taught me that one of my personal red flags, one of the things that would help me recognize that perhaps my heart might need checking, is when I feel I can't attend to someone because I'm too busy. Bad habit. And that's all it is, I have discovered. Because an open heart isn't really as much a matter of time as it is a matter of being present, available, and open to whomever is in my physical space at any given moment.

Several years ago I took my mother shopping for a winter coat. Shopping is not my favorite activity, and it was getting close to dinnertime before we finally found the right coat. It was a soft grey wool with raglan sleeves that hung way below her fingertips and a hem that brushed the tops of her shoes. The saleswoman sent for the alterations lady, who helped Mother onto the raised platform and went to work.

*I thank my great God that he has given us a portion of his Spirit to soften our hearts.*
ALMA 24:8

I sank into a chair in the corner of the fitting room, lost in my own little world, wondering if I had time on the way home to stop at the grocery store to pick up something for dinner.

Gradually, on the edges of my consciousness, I began to hear a conversation. Mother would ask a question, and the alterations lady would answer. At first the answers were rather brief, but as the questions and interest from Mother continued, the answers became longer. The woman's voice became more animated. By the time we left, the two of them were laughing together like old friends. And I was left out— a shriveled, self-absorbed, tired little soul in the corner. And withholding myself, I exited just as I had entered. I looked at Mother. She had come in just as weary as I but was leaving with an extra spring in her step.

Aha. Here was a discovery that I didn't recognize then, but when I began to experiment years later, I thought back on that afternoon and identified a process that is repeatable:

> *"Be not faithless, but believing." Believe in yourselves. Believe in your capacity to do some good in this world. God sent us here for a purpose, and that was to improve the world in which we live. The wonderful thing is that we can do it.*
>
> PRESIDENT
> GORDON B. HINCKLEY[6]

*Opening one's heart creates energy. Closing one's heart depletes energy.* As I sat in the corner of the dressing room with my little closed heart and thought about the list of things I still had to do, my fatigue increased. Mother looked down at the alterations lady and opened her heart by expressing an interest, and Mother's energy increased. "Do you like your job? How long have you worked here? What about your family? Where are

> *Open hearts create energy. Closed hearts deplete energy.*

> ———— ❧ ————
>
> *An open heart looks outward.*
>
> *A closed heart looks inward.*

> ———— ❧ ————
>
> *To the extent that we can come to see others differently, we can undergo a fundamental change, a change in our being, a change of our emotions and attitudes, a change of heart.*
>
> C. TERRY WARNER[7]

you from?" *An open heart looks outward. A closed heart looks inward.*

I learned something else about opening hearts from the coat-buying encounter. An open heart very often coaxes open someone else's closed heart. It's almost magical. An open heart presents a safe place that others sense, and they respond, sometimes immediately and sometimes much more slowly. No matter, however, whether they respond or not, because, in the meantime, *we* feel so much better living this way. Go ahead, experiment for yourself. That's what this is all about!

———— ❧ ————

### THE EXPERIMENT

1. I will be more aware of the condition of my **heart,** and with that awareness, seek to keep it more **open** toward others.

2. I will do this in **the normal course of my life,** in other

words, not feel pressured to put any extra activities into my day—no extra visits, casseroles, etc.

3. I will **notice the Spirit** and be willing to **honestly report** what happened or didn't happen. In doing so, I will try to understand my personal stumbling blocks and strengths.

Do these experimenting rules seem right to you, or would you like to modify them in some way? This is *your* experiment. Make it work for you.

Your modifications

_____

_____

_____

Caution: Don't set out to *do* anything differently. Observe the physical/emotional/spiritual response of your heart, independent of your words or actions. Awareness is the key.

Think of your own metaphor for a shriveled heart or an expanded heart. What image do you see that would be personally useful?

Observe your physical approach to people. What is your body language saying? If you feel yourself withdrawing, putting up a wall, change your physical position and notice if it causes you to feel differently.

Take the initiative to get outside yourself and express an interest in those you encounter. Pray for the courage to do so.

During some of your personal scripture time you might want to reread Alma's passages on experimentation (Alma 32), or you may want to look up scriptures that describe the heart in the Topical Guide.

# Chapter Three

# GOD'S LOVE

_Yea, it is the love of God,_

_which sheddeth itself abroad in the hearts of the children of men;_

_wherefore, it is the most desirable above all things._

_And he spake unto me, saying:_

_Yea, and the most joyous to the soul._

1 NEPHI 11:22–23

What is it that pries open a hardened heart? What enlarges and softens the most shriveled of human souls? What is the most desirable, the most delicious, the most joyous above all to the soul? That's easy to answer: It's being flooded with God's love, being awash with His profound acceptance and glory, being encircled and comforted and healed and set free to go and do!

Sister Smith was in that good part of her mission. She'd been out over a year, and let's face it, she knew how to do it.

She had settled into a predictable rhythm in her missionary schedule. The homesickness was over, the language was working for her, and daily anxieties were minimal. She had earned a certain reputation and acceptance among the other missionaries and the members. Life was good—good, that is, except for one troublesome relationship. And it wasn't even *always* troublesome. It was just that she was hoping to be of some help to another person who was obviously struggling and whom the mission president hoped she could help. Yes, there had been some good things happen, but on this particular day Sister Smith was feeling ineffective at best and a little jerked around at worst. She was discouraged and a bit annoyed about her perceived failure when she went in for her regularly scheduled interview with the mission president.

During the interview Sister Smith just let go and unloaded her frustrations concerning the difficulty. The president was kind, reassuring Sister Smith that she probably was doing far more good than she realized. He expressed his sympathy and continued confidence in her. And then he asked if she, Sister Smith, were feeling the love of God for herself, personally. Sister Smith said that the question seemed out of context but she just answered "Yes" in an automatic sort of way and let the interview go on. However, at the end of the interview, the president came back to the same question, asking it again. "Are *you* feeling the love of God, Sister Smith, for *you, personally?*"

She later told me, "This time I stopped for a second before I answered. I thought about it. He quietly continued to press me, 'How often? *Every day?*' I thought again and then I said rather quietly, 'Yes.'"

Now that's all of the story that I know. It's all that the sister missionary told me years later because what she wanted to talk about was the interesting question that came twice during the course of the interview: *"Are you feeling the love of God—that He loves you, personally?"* She wanted to talk about how thinking about the question and giving herself a chance to *feel* the question helped her heart to change from one of frustration and irritation to one of love and patience

> When filled with God's love, we can do and see and understand things that we could not otherwise do or see or understand. Filled with His love, we can endure pain, quell fear, forgive freely, avoid contention, renew strength, and bless and help others in ways surprising even to us.
>
> ELDER JOHN H. GROBERG[8]

and long-suffering. She was an obedient missionary. Her covenants were in place. All she needed to do was to ask for the ability to open her heart and then allow that to happen by opening herself to the love that God had for her. That simple adjustment changed everything. Almost instantly, she was better able to interact with someone who gave her so little nurturing, so little encouragement or support. Not only that, when she felt God's love for her, it filled her empty reservoir and her capacity to love everyone increased automatically. Gone were the feelings of being worn down and burned out.

> *Pray unto the Father with all the energy of heart, that ye may be filled with this love, which he hath bestowed upon all who are true followers of his Son, Jesus Christ.*
>
> MORONI 7:48

When Nephi asked for the interpretation of his father's dream, he was told that the tree represented "the love of God" (1 Nephi 11:22). That love was described as "most desirable above all things" and "the most joyous to the soul" (1 Nephi 11:22– 23). I've sometimes wondered if the phrase "love of God" means *our* love of God or *His* love of us. I'm no scholar of prepositional phrases in the scriptures, but my own experience has convinced me that it is impossible in all practicality to separate the two. When I feel His love for me I instantaneously am flooded with my love for Him and vice versa. We cannot have one without the other. No wonder it is always simply and profoundly stated "the love of God." Sometimes the scriptures even seem to indicate that Jesus Christ

Himself is "the love of God." Of course, the Savior would be the physical representation, the incarnate expression of God's love for us, and our acceptance of Him and our profound gratitude for His atoning sacrifice would be the ultimate expression of *our* love for the Father! The love of God is the heart of Christianity, the centerpiece of the plan of salvation, and opening our hearts to receive and give it is our daily opportunity.

> ———— 🐝 ————
>
> *God's love fills the immensity of space; therefore, there is no shortage of love in the universe, only in our willingness to do what is needed to feel it.*
>
> ELDER JOHN H. GROBERG[9]

The wonder of it all is that God loves us all of the time; however, our ability to *feel* His love comes and goes. It seems to be dependent on many things. By covenant, He promises that when we keep His commandments we will have His Spirit to be with us. I believe that, and my desire is to keep my covenants—both because He loves me and as my gift of love to Him. And so when I don't feel His love, am I failing to claim the blessings that are mine? I think so.

But I also know those who have broken their covenants, who have afterward been awakened and healed by His love. I think of a young man who told me his story. When he was about fifteen, going to church seemed to have less and less relevance to his life. And when he got a part-time job that often included a Sunday shift, it became even easier to miss meetings. Within about a year he had drifted into a morally difficult lifestyle and was unhappy and discouraged. He had difficulty sleeping and would often walk the streets in the earliest hours of the day. He told me he was doing just that at about 3 A.M. one morning when something happened. He said that it was sudden. He felt God's love surround him. He went home and got out his scriptures and began reading. Over a period of several months he basked and grew, fed by the influence of the Spirit. His life changed. He repented and returned to church. This boy's story may seem odd, even unfair when we read that we are required to keep the commandments in order to feel the Spirit, but God, in His infinite wisdom, knows how and when to succor us with His love. It is His to give and ours to accept in gratitude. It is part of the glorious and infinite gift of the Atonement.

I know that my ability to feel His love is dependent on many things besides my willingness to keep His commandments. Perhaps you are the same. That's where this experiment begins. Ask yourself the question: What can I do, beyond being obedient to the commandments and praying fervently, that will help me feel His love, personally, every day?

I know women who live in marriages or who are in contact with ex-husbands where there is constant criticism and pain. Who knows where the fault lies? In the name of self-preservation, they have learned to survive by protecting and hardening their own hearts. Even as they speak the right words and go through seemingly righteous motions, these unhappy people keep their shriveled hearts safely hidden behind protective walls. I understand this. It seems even wise at times. They have been wounded by their spouses and wish to protect themselves from further pain. But at the same time their hardened hearts also prevent them from feeling love from their Father in Heaven. And it is His love and peace that they so desperately crave.

> *But behold, he has brought them into his everlasting light, yea, into everlasting salvation; and they are encircled about with the matchless bounty of his love.*
>
> ALMA 26:15

I have seen others who carry great burdens, whose hearts are shriveled by the daily demands of poor health, critical needs of family members, desperate financial problems, and so many real crises—all of them creating a debilitating fear that keeps them focused inward until they just don't see anyone else. And yet paradoxically, the very looking outward, the reverencing of the Deity in others would open a space for God to step in and heal the wounds that continue to bleed in their own hearts.

*The fruit [of faith and patience], which is most precious, which is sweet above all that is sweet, and which is white above all that is white, yea, and pure above all that is pure; and ye shall feast upon this fruit even until ye are filled, that ye hunger not, neither shall ye thirst.*

Alma 32:42

I have a friend who was abused as a child. She felt stunted in her ability to love and be loved. She longed to be able to forgive and have her wounds healed, but it didn't happen. She prayed. She struggled. Then somehow she stumbled onto a new path. She told me that every time she experienced those feelings of being wounded, she would look around her for someone she might have wounded and reach out to them, trying to assuage their suffering even though she understood that she was partly to blame. She said that as she continued to do this, over time she felt the forgiveness, healing, and love that had evaded her for so long.

I am blessed, personally, beyond measure, and yet oddly enough, I, too, struggle to feel His love for me every day. When I stack my obstacles against others' they seem too frivolous to be authentic. And yet, this mortal existence is designed by a genius, so that we will all, no matter our circumstances or parentage or gifts, have to exercise our agency to come to Him. And so though my problems may seem small to an outsider, they are big enough for me to desperately need Him.

As you experiment I am sure that you will find many ways to increase your ability to feel His love. I found an unexpected one as I began to experiment.

Because I have been so obviously blessed, I haven't often been viewed as "needy" by many people. During the past few years I have been blessed by two new friends. Individually, and in different ways, they saw some needs that those who had known my husband and me longer hadn't seen or at least we had not allowed them to see. I was embarrassed, almost felt undressed, as these new friends quietly opened their hearts and began to attend to us. To receive such attention felt like such an identity shift. They were gentle and not intrusive, sending us little notes, visiting and chatting over a period of months and now years. While at first there was some discomfort (a bit of heart-hardening) on my part, I have come to see their concern and kindness as evidence of God's love for us. In fact, I feel His love with each encounter. And as I have identified, I now realize that when I need to feel more of His love in my life I count the kindnesses of others and realize that they are expressions of His love for me. This concept is so beautifully described in the words of a favorite hymn:

*Each life that touches ours for good*
*Reflects thine own great mercy, Lord;*
*Thou sendest blessings from above*
*Thru words and deeds of those who love.*[10]

I loved Christmas Eves when our children were small. Typically, my husband, Jim, would help me carry the presents out of the basement, fill the stockings, and then go to bed. In the quiet of the night I would spend a long time arranging and rearranging the children's Christmas gifts and picturing how each child would react to each one. In my imagination I could see them coming down the stairs in the morning. Their eyes were a window into souls that believed anything was possible. In fact, on Christmas morning, the impossible would materialize. In those solitary, early morning hours, I imagined their faces lighting up and anticipated their surprise and delight— the time they would spend putting each toy together and the good times they would have playing with it. I knew they would throw their arms around Jim and me with expressions of delight and gratitude. And it all happened many, many times, just as I had imagined in the quiet of those early morning hours of Christmas after Christmas.

One Christmas Eve, after the stockings were filled and the gifts had been arranged and rearranged in the chairs designated for each child, I remembered a gift that we had hidden in a storage building behind our house. It was long after midnight and snowing heavily. I put on boots, a warm coat, and gloves, then pulling a hat over my head, I stepped out into the night. After retrieving the box, I turned and retraced my steps, now filling in with fresh snow. Just as I was opening the kitchen door, I stopped. The still, white world pulled me back, and I quickly set the package inside and turned around. *My work is finished. I'll just take a short walk before I go to bed,* I thought to myself.

With the snow continuing to fall, I walked down the driveway and up the street and around the corner. Quiet became quieter and soft, softer. I walked deeper and deeper into the still beauty, down one side of the street and back on the other. The only lights in our neighbors' houses were eerily similar. One light on in the basement and one in the living room. Shadowy silhouettes would appear in the basement then disappear to appear again in the living room—parents silently preparing delight and fascination for their children. And there I stood, in a snow-filled world, filled with wonder at the enchantment pre-pared for me by my Father. Waves of love and gratitude washed over me.

My husband is a butterfly collector. Glasswings, Morphos, Parnasius, Colorado Hairstreaks—we have museum drawers full of outrageously unnecessary beauty. It is beauty that causes you to wonder how your vocabulary could be so small and woefully inadequate.

> *The overwhelming message of the Atonement is the perfect love the Savior has for each and all of us. It is a love which is full of mercy, patience, grace, equity, long-suffering, and, above all, forgiving.*
>
> PRESIDENT JAMES E. FAUST[11]

I think of the Savior and Michael and whoever else was doing the work during those days of Creation, thinking about us just as I thought of my little ones on Christmas Eve. The creators must have said, "Oh, wait until Virginia sees this Colorado Hair-streak. She won't believe how delicate the tails are and the exquisitely changing shades of purple. Certainly when she sees the beauty and the care we have taken with this creation she will know how much we love her, and she will spontaneously turn in wonder to us and let us flood her with our love!"

Yes. When I want to fill my heart with His love, I open my

eyes to the creations of His hand, especially the ones that seem outrageously and uselessly beautiful—sunsets, sunrises, ice crystals, patterns in drying mud, golden cottonwood leaves against red rock cliffs, the melancholy sound of the first cricket in August, moss-covered rocks in a mountain stream, the way a baby laughs before she can do useful things such as talking and walking.

We have a son and sons-in-law who love to play golf, so you can imagine their excitement when they had an opportunity several years ago to attend a golf clinic with a world-famous pro.

Golf bags jostling between them, the boys burst through the door into our family room on a late summer afternoon after the clinic.

Reporting the highlight of the day, James said: "We stood in a line and the pro went from person to person. He watched each person swing and then gave some pointers. When he came to me, he said: 'Basically, you've got a very good swing. But this time, when you swing back, extend a little further to the right and explode through the ball. Good,' he said. 'Practice that way. And if anyone ever tries to tell you differently, you tell them that I said you have a great swing!' Then he moved on to the next player, and I kept practicing."

"Did it work?" we asked.

"Not yet, but it will," he answered confidently.

As the boys went on through the room and out the door to do a little more practicing in the backyard, I felt a twinge of envy.

Wouldn't it be nice if there were someone whom I trusted that much—an expert who could take a look at my life and say: "Basically, you're doing great. But if you would just do this one little thing, it would make a big difference"?

All at once the light turned on! I have those kinds of experts. I have prophets, living and dead, who speak in general conference and from the pages of my scriptures. And I have the Holy Ghost to personalize their messages to my exact, immediate, and individual needs.

One of the remarkable qualities about God's love for us is that not only do we experience it as validating and affirming, but it also produces **growth** and **change** in us. It literally moves us forward, toward Him and our own eventual exaltation. It is a sculpting, correcting, and purposeful kind of love.

That sounds so threatening because we all have received criticism and correction from those who love imperfectly—who may love in a manipulative and a selfish kind of way. So many times our love becomes a way to get people to do what we think they should do. That kind of shaping is most often resented, discouraging, debilitating, and not at all motivating.

I have thought about my own personal experiences. Though I have sometimes left a church meeting feeling profoundly discouraged about my own progress after listening to someone's lesson or talk, I don't believe I have ever closed my softly worn, leather-bound scriptures deeply discouraged. That is not to say that I leave the scriptures feeling perfect. Far from it. In fact, in my scripture reading I often come upon verses that show me clearly where I need to repent and change—over and over again. In other words, what I need to do to improve my swing. But along with that I also hear repeated in a most credible and comforting way, "Basically, you've got a very good swing, and if anyone ever tries to tell you differently, you tell them that I said you have a great swing!" The scriptures motivate and energize me in my quest to change and become better.

So, when I want to feel His love for me more fully, I do whatever it takes to stay in the words of the prophets. I keep my general conference issue of the *Ensign* open. I keep my scriptures open. And I keep my heart open because His love enters through the words of His prophets, validated and personalized by the Holy Ghost. And then I act. I do whatever I feel nudged to do. I review my covenants. I live them more completely. And I have started the cycle of giving and receiving love.

When I try to describe how I feel when I experience God's love for me I am overwhelmed by His generosity. I like to think of the words that describe how I feel when I experience His love. They include:

Acknowledged, accepted

Validated, noticed

Cared for, supported

Encouraged, uplifted

Motivated, inspired

Comforted, healed

Nourished, nurtured

Changed, more confident, more able

Very often when I leave my house in the early morning dark and start up the street to meet my walking friends, I pray. My prayers are most often about the day ahead—the schedule, my responsibilities, the pressing needs of my family or other specifics—but sometimes my morning prayer is a simple but energetic plea: "Let me feel Thy love for me—let me feel that light coming from your smiling and stabilizing generosity." I need to *really feel* that *my* name is engraved on the palms of His hands. I ask my Father in Heaven to soften, open, and enlarge my heart, to fill it with His love.

I have sometimes experienced a warm, quiet, comforting feeling flood over me in response to my prayer. More often it is less tangible. But no matter because just the asking has given me a different direction and new sustenance. I am ready to be obedient, to conform my life to His will, not mine. Just the asking has refocused me and has softened my

*Behold, I have graven thee upon the palms of my hands; thy walls are continually before me.*
ISAIAH 49:16

heart and readied it to receive love, perhaps through a lovingly prepared meal, an overdo apology haltingly delivered, a butterfly on the wing, a thumbs up, or a voice within that says that I've got a basically good swing and that I'm going to make it after all.

Knowing how it feels when I experience His love is so important, and knowing what I can do to increase the frequency of that feeling is important because my capacity to experience His love is the model for how well I love others.

Think of your desire to feel His love. As a true follower of Christ, pray fervently to be filled with it.

Take time, right now, to think of the ways you have experienced His love throughout the past week. Glance back through the preceding chapter to get yourself started. Allow yourself to be filled with gratitude for these very specific and personal manifestations of His love for you.

If you have been or are the victim of someone else's hardened heart, put that person aside and honestly evaluate your own heart. Has your heart shriveled in response? Would you consider experimenting? It might be too much—at first—when interacting with those who have hurt you, but you might find that your closed, defensive heart assumes that *everyone and everything* are instruments of pain rather than love. No need to rush into this. Just consider it.

# Chapter Four

# EXTENDING GOD'S LOVE TO OTHERS

———— ❧ ————

*I receive you to fellowship,*
*in a determination that is fixed,*
*immovable, and unchangeable,*
*to be your friend and brother through the grace of God*
*in the bonds of love,*
*to walk in all the commandments of God*
*blameless, in thanksgiving,*
*forever and ever.*

D&C 88.133

Long, long ago, we all sat together in a grand council in heaven while our loving Father described His plan to us. We surely understood it more fully than we do now and we must have understood more about our relationship with one another. We knew that we were family. We *really* knew it. We

*We help others feel God's love
when we are:
Supportive, encouraging,
inspiring, nourishing,
nurturing, comforting,
compassionate, understanding,
patient, long-suffering,
good-humored, willing to cut
him/her some slack and
extend the benefit of the
doubt, willing to talk and
listen openly and honestly,
trusting and accepting/
nonjudgmental when we
counsel, guide, teach, mentor,
pray and fast with, empower,
validate, acknowledge,
withhold judgment.*

had experience with one another. We loved one another. We felt responsible for one another. Elder John A. Widtsoe paints this picture for us:

In our pre-existent state, in the day of the great council, we made a certain agreement with the Almighty. The Lord proposed a plan, conceived by him. We accepted it. Since the plan is intended for all men, we became parties to the salvation of every person under that plan. We agreed, right then and there, to be not only saviors for ourselves, but measurably saviors for the whole human family. We went into a partnership with the Lord. The working out of the plan became then not merely the Father's work, and the Savior's work, but also our work. The least of us, the humblest, is in partnership with the Almighty in achieving the purpose of the eternal plan of salvation. That places us in a very responsible attitude towards the human race.[12]

My friends from India greet each other by bringing their hands together, bowing slightly, and saying the word, *Namaste.* It means, roughly translated, "I honor the Deity within you." That is precisely what we do when we open our hearts to another; we honor the fact that he or she, like us, is a child of the same loving Father, worthy of all respect and careful attention.

> *We cannot help others feel God's love when we are: Irritated, critical, discouraged, annoyed, self-absorbed, angry, indignant, or filled with self-pity, hostility, or bitterness.*

Several years ago I visited some of the newly renovated historical sites in Kirtland, Ohio. I was particularly anxious to see the room where the School of the Prophets convened. I knew something of the grand and glorious things that had occurred in that room, the lofty ideas that were studied, the noble men who had participated in the school. My expectations were high. When we arrived at the Newell K. Whitney Store, the guides directed us to a steep staircase behind the counter of the restored general store. We climbed it, so narrow that our shoulders nearly touched each wall, to find that it opened into a tiny room about 8x10 feet, its only furnishings a potbellied stove and several very narrow, very low, backless benches. Confronting such austerity, I was taken aback. I had in my mind the grand ideas that had been discussed in the room and what was before me was shockingly sparse and small.

> *I wish that we could feel that brotherly love continued, and that it was spreading and increasing, flowing from the fountain of life—from God—from heart to heart as oil is poured from vessel to vessel, that harmony, sympathy, kindness and love might be universal among us.*
>
> PRESIDENT JOHN TAYLOR[13]

About twenty men had crowded onto those narrow benches in 1833. The school began at sunrise and usually went until late afternoon. Each morning the teacher was instructed to arrive before the students (Orson Hyde during January and February of 1833) to prepare himself and the room. The environment for learning certainly was not created by the physical appointments, but it was created by the attitudes and rituals. I believe we could label these "open-heart" attitudes and rituals. As each man entered he reaffirmed his commitment and goodwill by exchanging a formal salutation with the teacher. That greeting is found in Doctrine & Covenants section 88 and its ritualistic nature may seem a little strange in our twenty-first century world, but verse 133 is rich with meaning. The teacher is instructed to salute his brother or brethren with these words:

> I salute you in the name of the Lord Jesus Christ, in token or remembrance of the everlasting covenant, in which covenant I receive you to fellowship, in a determination that is **fixed, immovable, and unchangeable, to be your friend and brother** through the grace of God in the bonds of love, **to walk in all the commandments of God** blameless, in thanksgiving, forever and ever. Amen.

Then the one so greeted answered with the same salutation. Can you imagine a learning environment built on such an affirmation of love and commitment from and to your fellow students? Can you imagine the personal safety they must have felt—and the energy that would otherwise have been used to defend and protect themselves and was now available for them to learn and grow and change? Can you imagine the power of the Holy Ghost in a room where each participant had vowed to be a friend and brother through the grace of God and in the bonds of love? These men studied everything from theology to grammar. Their questions were honest, their hearts were open, and they were willing and able to learn from one another and from the Lord.

> *Now, as ye are desirous to come into the fold of God, and to be called his people, and are willing to bear one another's burdens, that they may be light; Yea, and are willing to mourn with those that mourn; yea, and comfort those that stand in need of comfort.*
> MOSIAH 18:8–9

I believe that our ability to worship God, to reaffirm our covenants and receive the healing power of the Holy Ghost, to receive the instruction we need in order to make personal progress—all of these things are greatly affected by how secure and safe we feel in our Church environment during the three-hour block of time on Sundays. If we have to spend our energy dealing with feelings that we are not accepted, being concerned about our appearance, or worrying that what we do or say will be judged harshly, in other words that the fellowship of our ward members is anything but "fixed, immovable, and unchangeable," we certainly won't be able to make the kind of progress we could make otherwise.

In today's world we don't greet one another at the doors of our chapels or in the neighborhood or at general conference with a formal salutation, but could we not pray on a Sunday morning for a softened heart, for a heart that is open to others, for a heart that is willing to let others learn on our time?

Let's return to that premortal grand council and the agreement we entered into with the Almighty. How am I to meet my responsibility to be a savior for the whole human family? What tools can I use in fulfilling this daunting mission? I cannot use the methods that Lucifer would use. They would include coercion, control, force, manipulation, deceit, and other power tricks. My partnership is with the Lord. I will have to learn to do it His way. I will have to use His tools, the chief one being love.

Remember how we feel when we experience His love?

Acknowledged, accepted
Validated, noticed
Cared for, supported
Encouraged, uplifted
Motivated, inspired
Comforted, healed
Nourished, nurtured
Changed, more confident, more able

Those are precisely the ways we want others to feel when they are with us!

Many years ago—so many that my husband and I and our six children still "owned" our own center row in the chapel— my young daughter leaned over to me and asked if she could go across the aisle and sit next to Sister Hutchings. I absently said, "Yes, but just wait until the sacrament's finished."

The last deacon had barely touched the bench when Heidi slipped over to our little neighbor who sat alone on a side bench. Tiny Sister Hutchings scooped Heidi up in one arm as if she were one of the bouquets of sweet peas that she regularly delivered around the neighborhood from her bounteous garden. She whispered in her ear, and Heidi's face brightened in reply. After church, running to catch up with us, Heidi shouted breathlessly, "Guess what, Mom? Sister Hutchings said that she was praying all during the sacrament that someone would come and sit by her. And I did!"

I was touched that Heidi had been prompted and had acted on the prompting. But it was not until our children had grown and left the ward that I understood Sister Hutchings' prayer. Who would have thought that this woman, a woman at the historic and spiritual center of our ward, would be praying to feel acknowledged, validated and accepted through something as simple as having someone choose to sit with her in sacrament meeting?

Decades have passed since that little incident, and like Sister Hutchings, my husband and I no longer have a particular row that the congregation knows belongs to us by virtue of our large family. Sometimes my husband has other commitments, and I find myself alone, looking for a place to sit. It's a little risky. I might walk down the aisle of the chapel from row to row only to be told that there isn't room, or I might sit on a row alone, wondering

> *The kingdom of God is like a besieged city surrounded on all sides by death. Each man has his place on the wall to defend and no one can stand where another stands, but nothing prevents us from calling encouragement to one another.*
>
> MARTIN LUTHER[14]

if anyone will sit by me. Others might see me sitting alone and think I am "saving a place" for someone else. When I have occasion to sit on the stand or in the choir seats, I find myself watching this process—the often uncertain, tentative way some members come into the chapel alone. I am delighted when without hesitation people move over when someone inquires if

there is room for one more. It seems to me that there should
*always* be room for one more.

I particularly love it when people come into a chapel or
church classroom and break that invisible barrier around someone who is sitting alone, asking if they may sit with them. Most
of us sit alone, not because we wish to be alone, but because we
don't want to intrude where we may not be wanted. We can be
quite sure that someone sitting alone won't be offended if we
ask to sit with her or him. When we choose to sit with others it
is a simple way of extending God's acknowledging love. This
simple act validates their very existence and lets them know that
we welcome their presence in our lives. It is a very big deal and
takes so little from us. I can see why Sister Hutchings found it
worth praying for and why Heidi celebrated all the way home.
They, together, were sharing God's love.

Sheri Dew told me a simple but wonderful story about the
last encounter she had with my mother before Mom's death.
Sheri and my sister were working on something together and
needed a piano and so had gone over to my parents' apartment
to use theirs. Mother was in the other room visiting with her
siblings. Sheri and Kathy went to work on the piano, laughing
and talking their way through the process. In the middle of
their work, Mother and her guests came through the room on

their way to the front door. Mother's wobbly steps were matched by her brother's sure ones as she held onto his arm. She was thanking them for coming to see her when she reached a spot directly behind Sheri and Kathy. Without a break in her gait, Mother looked directly toward Sheri and pointing with her free hand, said, "I like that girl!" Without waiting for a response she kept tottering through the room. When Sheri told me this story she said that she chuckled to herself all the way back to her office. In fact, she fairly danced all the way, so validated, accepted, encouraged, and loved, did she feel. When we truly pay attention to others—with open hearts, hearts filled with His validating, acknowledging, and accepting love—we work miracles when we simply pass it on.

After I began experimenting with opening my heart and as I became more aware of what God's love feels like, I quickly began to rethink people in my life who seemed to be very good at loving the way our Heavenly Father loves—those who consistently helped me feel the feelings I am describing in this chapter.

I was in my early thirties, expecting our sixth child, when I called my friend Phyllis one day. She was twenty-something-years my senior, a neighbor, and ward member. She was on my list to call on some Relief Society business, the nature of which

I have long ago forgotten. But I have not forgotten what she said when I finished my business. I was about to hang up and go on to the next number when she asked, "Virginia, are you all right?"

"What do you mean?" I said.

"You just sound tired," she said with a kindness that wrapped around me like a mother's arms.

"Oh," I said, talking through the tears that were suddenly choking my words. "I'm such a mess," I snuffled as I tried to explain how over-whelmed I felt.

She listened for a minute and then rescued me so I could keep crying for a few more minutes. "Why don't you and Jim take a couple of days off and go up to our cabin? That would give you a rest."

Finally I could talk again. "Oh, Phyllis. Thanks so much, but I don't think it'd work. It's not getting away I need. I just need to be in my house without so many people. I'm so behind. If I got away it would just be worse when I got back." Snuffle, snuffle. "But don't worry, I'll be okay. And thanks, Phyllis."

"Okay, but you know that the offer's good anytime."

> *Sameness is to be found most among the most "natural" men, not among those who surrender to Christ. How monotonously alike all the great tyrants and conquerors have been; how gloriously different are the saints.*
>
> C. S. LEWIS[15]

Phyllis's ability to hear my fatigue, and to care for and support me, was genuine and spontaneous. Even though she offered her cabin, it wasn't what I needed. She gave me the thing I needed—just an expression of concern, a moment of comfort, a word of encouragement. She had opened her heart and extended God's love to me. All I remember from that encounter was the feeling of being encircled in someone's arms, being held onto, being held up. Isn't that what the Savior has promised us and isn't that what we have promised Him we will do for each other?

You don't need to withhold your comfort and support because you don't have the time or capacity to move permanently into the center of someone else's life. I believe that sometimes I hesitate to open my heart and extend unreserved love because I truly believe I would then be obligated to take in the orphan, adopt and rear him to adulthood. When examined, of course, that is foolish, but emotionally it is the premise I work on, and my immediate response is to move my heart back, tighten it up a bit, build a wall, and say the expected words, which lack the accompanying reality of God's love. Contrary to my emotionally held belief, most of the time, all others usually need from me, and all I usually need from others—and even from the Lord—is simply to be held and encircled with love while I cry a little. Then I can hang up the phone, blow my nose, and go back to work.

My mother told a story that I love because it illustrates so simply a way we can extend love.

> Some years ago I had a friend who decided at the age of fifty that she was going to learn to play the piano. She courageously started out with *Thompson's Book I.* Each morning she went to the church at seven o'clock, where she would practice on the piano and the organ. After about a year they asked her to play a special number for one of the Relief Society lessons. She said she didn't feel ready, to give her another three months. The three months passed, and she consented to play a special number that she had memorized. This was her first public appearance on the piano. She started out beautifully. It went well for about three measures; then she lost it. Everything went blank. Her music teacher, who was present, said, "Don't be ruffled, Merle. Just start over." She started over and made it all the way through without a single mistake.
>
> We have never loved Merle like we loved her that

morning. Perhaps it was because she faltered a little in the beginning and we were all pulling for her, saying to ourselves, "Come on, Merle, you can do it."[16]

You and I feel this spiritual encouragement so often in ordinary Relief Society meetings. Sit back and notice it when you have a chance. I did last week. As the teacher moved through her lesson, the sisters became more and more involved in the topic. We could feel the teacher extending herself, even risking a bit. And then I could literally feel the other sisters in the room leaning forward spiritually, working with and helping one another learn and grow together. It was no small miracle because this lending of spirits allowed God's love to permeate the room. I looked around in wonder, knowing that this might just be the same atmosphere that Joseph and the others enjoyed in the School of the Prophets.

> *[See that] ye have purified your souls in obeying the truth through the Spirit unto unfeigned love of the brethren, see that ye love one another with a pure heart fervently.*
>
> 1 PETER 1:22

Some assumptions have to be made if I choose to freely extend love to others. If I honor the Deity within others and my divine connection to them—brothers and sisters who sat together in the grand council, pledging to help each other—it seems that I have to be willing to assume a certain amount of goodness in every person right away. Someone once told me that when she works with adolescents whose behavior might be irritating to others, she always "assumes nobility of intent." I like that phrase. Behavior isn't always noble, but it is easy for me to believe that people generally mean well, even if their actions don't entirely reflect their desires. And if I go into relationships assuming that intentions are noble it is easier for me to extend love and non-judgmental acceptance. I believe we should exercise good judgment about our own personal safety and our emotional health, but I know that I am happier if I assume goodness and nobility of purpose in others. In fact, there is no other way that I can keep my heart softened and open and filled with God's love.

> *Above our mantel is engraved: "There isn't anyone you couldn't love Once you've heard their story."*
> MARY LOU KOWNACKI[17]

Elder Boyd K. Packer once shared his decision to "assume nobility of intent." He wrote:

A few years ago I indulged on one occasion in some introspection and found there were reasons why I didn't like myself very well. Foremost among them was the fact that I was suspicious of some I met. I had in mind this thought: "What's his angle? What's he going to try to do?" This came about because I had been badly used by someone I trusted. Cynicism and bitterness were growing within. I determined to change and made a decision that I would trust everyone. I have tried to follow that rule since. If someone is not worthy of trust, it is his responsibility to show it—not mine to find out. . . .

As I begin a new relationship . . . it is on the basis of confidence and trust. I have been much happier since. Of course, there have been times when I have been disappointed, and a few times when I have been badly used. I do not care about that. Who am I not to be so misused or abused? Why should I be above that? If that is the price of extending trust to everyone, I am glad to pay it.[18]

One of the great wonders of God's love is that it expresses itself uniquely through each person's personality. My friend Mary was a bright, articulate, and forthright woman. About fifteen years older than I, she was not only a friend but a valued mentor. Mary always spoke directly and to the point, but because her motives were so pure, I always received her counsel as messages of God's love. She absolutely loved the Lord and His work, and along with that she loved me and expected a lot of me.

In short, she assumed that I could do whatever the Lord asked me to do. One day as she was rehearsing an Easter program in which I had a speaking part, she kept telling me to be a bit more dramatic than I was used to being. Finally, she stopped me mid-sentence, and putting her hands on her hips and placing her feet solidly apart she said, "Wait a minute everybody." Then, turning to me she asked a question that was really a statement, "Are you afraid of looking foolish, Virginia?"

"Well, yes, Mary, actually, I am," I responded, relieved that she had finally figured it out and hoping that she would now quit pushing me.

"Well," she chuckled, as if that were the easiest and most delightful diagnosis possible. "You need to get over that. You see, I grew up in a little branch where my family did just about everything—every lesson, sacrament meeting, program, everything—and my dad, who was the branch president, of course, taught us that if you're doing something for the Lord, just give it everything you have, and you don't need to worry about what other people think! Now let's do it again, and this time, do it for the Lord."

I know it was His love that Mary was extending to me because I suddenly felt more able, more confident, motivated, and inspired.

I was a counselor in the Relief Society presidency when Mary was a teacher. We were putting the hymnbooks on the chairs when she swept into the room on the day of her lesson.

"Who's conducting?" she asked.

"I am," I responded.

She looked me directly in the eye and said, "Virginia, *don't take my time!*"

I laughed out loud but was smart enough to watch the clock very carefully while giving the announcements.

> *A great secret of success is to go through life as a man who never gets used up . . . I still remain convinced that truth, love, peaceableness, meekness, and kindness are the violence which can master all other violence . . . All the kindness which a man puts out into the world works on the heart and the thoughts of mankind.*
>
> ALBERT SCHWEITZER[19]

I am recounting this incident because open-hearted encounters aren't all about sweet affirming words, they are about open hearts and they have to do with motives. Only Mary and I could be sure of those. I believe that Mary's motives in this case were about her devotion to the principles of her lesson and the women who were in the audience who had come to learn those principles. I could feel her respect and love for me and her acknowledgment of my position as a counselor. I felt *motivated* to "do it right." I felt *able* "to do it right." What might have sounded like a chastisement to someone standing nearby was to me a blanket of empowering love.

> O ye Corinthians, our mouth is open unto you, our heart is enlarged.
>
> 2 CORINTHIANS 6:11

Learning to live with an open heart is not about learning to say the right words and refraining from saying the wrong words. In fact, just the opposite. I would venture to say that when my heart is open and filled with God's love, I *cannot* say it wrong, and when it is hardened and closed to Him, I simply *cannot* say it right, no matter how carefully I may choose the words or phrases or inflections of voice. Remember that this is all about *becoming,* not *doing* or *saying.*

At the age of sixty-one, my friend Mary was diagnosed with pancreatic cancer and was gone within five weeks. I sat beside her bed and listened to her talk about her impending death with the same direct faith she had always demonstrated. How I loved that woman!

But I have told you all of this as an introduction to a day in my life more than ten years after her death. It was the first part of December, and I had been called as a ward Relief Society president a few weeks earlier.

It was one of those days when the commitments and pressures of my life were squeezing me from all sides. Christmas was fast approaching, and I had not even begun decorating or buying anything—not one garland was out of the storage room, not a single gift was in the trunk of my car. Our youngest child was due to come home after two years in the mission field, and there wasn't even a place for him to sleep. We had given his bed to a grandchild, and his room was stacked high with the residue of two-years' worth of my paper projects. The carpet and the wallpaper were being replaced in the living room, and furniture was stacked in the entrance hall and the dining room. You couldn't even get in the front door. As a newly called Relief Society presidency, we had a social and a Christmas program just around the corner, and we had kept too much of the planning of both of them in our own hands; consequently, there were loose ends trailing as far as the eye could see.

On this particular morning, as I made a list of the things I had to do and started driving from place to place with one eye on the road and another on my watch, the distress went far beyond the list of things to do. It had become more a list about my own basic worth. You see, it became startlingly clear that I couldn't do all the things people expected me to do, not because I had planned poorly, but because I just was not enough of a person to do them. I was ready to concede that I simply didn't have what it takes. As I drove, the tears started to run down my face. And most especially tears about my inadequacy and hopelessness as a Relief Society president. If I couldn't put on the socials and the Sunday meetings, how could I hope to minister and comfort and do the really important things? What made the bishop or anyone else think I could do this!?

At about this point in the drama there entered, stage right, my friend Mary. It was as if she popped into the passenger seat beside me.

And do you know what Mary said to me—directly over my right shoulder? It wasn't a big long speech or an argument. All she said—and she said it so clearly that I could actually hear her matter-of-fact tone of voice—all she said was: "Of course you can do it, Virginia! Of course you can!" And no matter where I went the rest of the day, she went with me, and I kept hearing her say those words. I heard her repeat them until I honestly believed they were true.

Mary had extended God's love to me for over a decade of her life, always helping me to feel more capable, more confident, motivated, and encouraged. In life, she had mentored and taught me so well that I could hear her beyond the grave on a day when my own heart was failing and I needed to feel His affirming, supporting, comforting, encouraging, nonjudgmental, empowering, enabling, encircling love.

A friend who is divorced spoke one day about the period of time when her marriage was beginning to unravel—the time before anything was public—when everything looked good on the outside, when no one suspected that anything was wrong, but when nothing was in fact right. She said everything was painful, especially coming to church.

> *Each of us, from time to time, is mentored and has chances to mentor. In my experience, truthful and caring one-liners that occur within such nurturing relationships have a long shelf life! You can probably recount three or four examples of how people have said something—probably a sentence or clause—and you remember it still. It moves and touches you still. Such has been the case with me.*
> ELDER NEAL A. MAXWELL[20]

"What could we at church have done for you that would have made it easier?" someone asked. She didn't hesitate when she responded. "All I wanted, all I needed, was for people to be kind. There was so little kindness in my life."

No one could have known that she had special needs. She looked on the outside as if everything were okay. And yet it wasn't. Think about it. She could be the person seated beside you on the bus, working in your office, or driving the neighborhood carpool. You and I cannot possibly know the hidden pain eating holes in individual lives, so if we want to be saviors, in partnership with the Lord, we will be kind to everyone, everywhere, all of the time.

> *Be the living expression of God's kindness: kindness in your face, kindness in your eyes, kindness in your smile, kindness in your warm greeting.*
> MOTHER TERESA[21]

Jot down the names of some people you know who consistently seem to affirm, validate, motivate, and nourish those around them. Look beyond family and close friends. Think about ward members, neighbors, coworkers. Is it the words they say, or is it something more powerful? Think of a specific encounter with such a person. Write or tell someone about it.

Take the opportunity TODAY to acknowledge, support,

and extend kindness to *everyone* you encounter. As you interact with them, don't pay attention to the words you say, pay attention instead to how you feel about them. Look outward. Concentrate on being open and respectful and interested. Are you metaphorically "cheering" for them?

*Chapter Five*

# THE RECIPROCITY OF OPEN HEARTS

———— ❧ ————

*I long to see you, . . .*
*that I may be comforted together with you*
*by the mutual faith both of you and me.*

ROMANS 1:11–12

I almost wish that we members of the Church didn't use the term *Mutual* to designate the weekday coming together of young men and young women because the common usage of the word has resulted in a loss of some of its rich meaning. So, for a moment, will you let go of the name "Mutual" and explore with me the word *mutual* with a small lowercase "m"? It means having the same feelings one for another, a kinship, or being directed toward one another or a like interest; it suggests a kind of intimacy or sharing of sentiments. Think of the phrases "mutual admiration" or "mutually attracted."

They both seem to suggest a kind of equality; a give-and-take; an openness. The word *reciprocal* fits in nicely with *mutual.*

The word *charity* sometimes conjures up an image of those who have, giving to those who have not, doing "alms" as rich people who in a noblesse-oblige sort of way, condescendingly give to those who are needy, gratefully reminding themselves how lucky they are not to be poor. This is not the true meaning of charity, not the scriptural meaning of charity. If charity is in fact "the pure love of Christ" (Moroni 7:47), then there is no sense of one person being more elevated than another, because we are all needy before God, all dependent on Him; and with that paradigm, we ought to behave with a kind of mutuality, reciprocity, and equality toward one another, rather than an attitude of "Big Me–Little You." Even as we give, we know that we receive. Paul suggested that reality when he said, "But by an equality, that now at this time your abundance may be a supply for their want, that their abundance also may be a supply for your

> *But by an equality, that now at this time your abundance may be a supply for their want, that their abundance also may be a supply for your want: that there may be equality.*
> 2 Corinthians 8:14

want: *that there may be equality*" (2 Corinthians 8:14; emphasis added).

Mutuality and reciprocity both fit with the open-heart experiment because inevitably, when you and I open our hearts to allow love to flow toward others, we simultaneously allow others to enter into our hearts—to see where we really live. It's a reciprocal deal!

Perhaps it is easiest to illustrate this negatively. Let's say that you have an acquaintance who at every encounter asks you lots of questions, wanting to know what you think and feel. He may listen carefully and seem intensely interested, and you respond by opening your soul. This all seems quite affirming and healthy unless, after multiple encounters over an extended period of time, you discover that this person is unwilling to open himself to you. When you inquire about him, perhaps he changes the subject or finds other ways to let you know that he intends to guard his inner self, and yet he expects you to remain transparent. When that happens, you can't help feeling a little exploited, and it makes it impossible to establish a trusting relationship. It definitely doesn't help you to relax and move your softened heart out from behind its protective wall.

So, if you want your encounters to be all about someone else and never want to share *your* real self, then perhaps this isn't the experiment for you. Remember that one of the main reasons for hardening and moving your heart back into your chest wall is to protect yourself and your own vulnerabilities from being discovered by another. So, having an open heart means that it's okay for others to see that you have your own struggles and triumphs. In fact, knowing this about you validates and blesses and inspires me in my own struggles.

> _Charity: The highest, noblest, strongest kind of love, not merely affection; the pure love of Christ. It is never used [in the scriptures] to denote alms or deeds or benevolence, although it may be a prompting motive._
>
> BIBLE DICTIONARY, 632

My mother lived this principle of mutuality beautifully and effortlessly. Her interest and concern were always directed to others, never pushing herself or her own stories forward. Yet she was willing to be absolutely open about herself when asked. This willingness to show her own vulnerabilities was perhaps her greatest gift to members of the Church who knew her personally or through her written words.

After her death, our family was approached with a request to publish a selection of letters Mother had written to family members. We wondered at the appropriateness of doing so. We had three concerns: first, we didn't want to be seen as exploiting her life for profit; second, we wondered how she would feel about making letters public that were written with the intention that they were private; and third, the letters seemed to be such a chronicle of ordinariness that we wondered if they would be useful or interesting to anyone except to family.

The first concern was easy to address: all revenues would be assigned to the Church Missionary Book of Mormon Fund. The second concern was also easily dismissed. We simply asked ourselves the question: "Would Mother feel as if her privacy were invaded? Would she care?" The answer was instantly, "No." Although she was always surprised that anyone would be interested, she was always willing to simply be who she was under any and all circumstances—public or private. She never pretended to be something she wasn't or tried to hide what she was. As we realized this, we also realized that her openness— her honest sharing of her day-to-day relationships with those nearest to her—might be important and useful to others. And so *Letters* by Marjorie Pay Hinckley was published a few months after her death.

Not too long afterward I went with my daughter and her children to a museum. It was a school holiday, and the interactive part of the museum was alive with children. I sat down to keep an eye on a couple of those who belonged to us when I noticed a young and very pregnant mother on a sofa in the corner reading a book. It was *Letters.* I watched her for a few minutes, noticing that she was about three-quarters of the way through. When she looked up in response to my gaze, I said, "Those are my mother's letters."

"What?" she said.

I stood up, walked the few steps to the sofa, and sat down next to her. "Sister Hinckley. She's my mother," I repeated, pointing to the little book in her hand.

Tears immediately filled her eyes, and words tumbled on top of each other, "I love her. I mean, every night I read just a little bit. I can't tell you how it keeps me going!"

"How?" I pressed. "We thought it would be boring to people who don't know the family—all the names and everything, but it looks like you've made it almost to the end."

"Oh," she said, wiping her tears away. "It makes me feel normal. She's so real. The letters are so honest. I mean, she did all the things that I'm doing, and it makes me feel like I'm going to make it after all. Sometimes I'm just so tired and bogged down with the kids and everything, and she makes me laugh. And even though she's funny and everything, you can tell that she really believes. It makes me want to keep going."

In fact, for all of us it is this open-hearted affirmation that my life is the same as yours that moves us forward much faster than when we believe that others' lives are orderly and peaceful and only ours is difficult and chaotic and full of bumps.

I have included the following thank-you letter, which my husband, Jim, and I received some time ago. The open-hearted writer helped Jim to feel God's love as she thanked him for his gift to her, a sharing of scriptures—scriptures he offered because they were so helpful to him in a time of adversity. So they were given from an open/self-disclosing heart. And they were received in the same way, as she allowed us to see her heart, her struggle to have faith in the midst of difficulty. It was impossible to feel the sincerity of her expressions without feeling encouraged in our own lives. As she so honestly described

*At BYU a fireside was held in which Marjorie [Hinckley] was featured with her daughters presenting incidents in her life. She had the audience of some twelve thousand in the palm of her hand. They chuckled throughout the evening at her refreshing sense of humor and jumped to their feet in a standing ovation at the conclusion. Later she expressed amazement at the response. My husband said, "Marge, they loved you because you were so relaxed and just yourself." "I couldn't think of anyone else to be!" she quickly responded.*

EVELYN P. HENRIKSEN[22]

her desire to thwart Satan by feeding her spiritual self, we couldn't help but be encouraged to do the same. This letter is a courageous expression of a woman's willingness to be vulnerable—to open her heart, and in so doing to unknowingly inspire and help others.

Dear Jim and Virginia,

Thank you, Jim, for the scriptures you shared with me today. I read and reread them all. How fitting they are for me and for the way I am feeling. It is embarrassing to know that lately I have neglected the obvious and succumbed to my weaknesses—negative thinking and dwelling on problems at hand. These have been crowding out the favorite parts of my life and seem to be where Satan knows he can tempt me with success. When I do attend to my inner needs and let "feeding" my spiritual self be my highest priority I seem able to keep my perspective closer to the Lord's. I have a testimony of the power of prayer and how it enables us to express gratitude as well as link us to the Lord's will in our lives. However, when I become overtaxed I tend to resist discovering the Lord's will, in case it will be too difficult to follow. In reading these scriptures I was again reminded of whose hands my life is in. The real difficulty will be if I don't listen. There is such strength in believing these messages. I know this is true, but if I don't keep saying it out loud and over and over again it gets lost in the worries of the day.

I want to repent and put my life more in line with the Lord's will because I have a feeling that I will be very sorry if I do not. Satan is truly out to get me lately. I can feel it. With your very loving support and help I will more likely remember to include the Lord in my every thought.

*We are lonesome animals. We spend all our life trying to be less lonesome. One of our ancient methods is to tell a story, begging the listener to say—and to feel—"Yes, that's the way it is, or at least that's the way I feel it. You're not as alone as you thought."*

JOHN STEINBECK[23]

I especially love D&C 98:3. I truly believe that all things I have been afflicted with will work for my good as well as the Lord's glory. I am so grateful to you both. I am so grateful for the Lord's patience with me and can hardly wait to see what's next.

Thank you for your prayers. I feel loved. All is well.

This letter was inspiring to us. After reading it, we wanted more than ever to exercise faith in the midst of adversity. You see, when I feel you struggling to meet your daily challenges with faith, I am encouraged that maybe I can do the same. When you are willing to share your stories—the refining fires of your lives—I take heart.

*When we risk sharing our real feelings, we develop relationships of understanding and trust. For we cannot really care or be cared for, love or be loved, understand or be understood, unless we are willing to open our treasures of time, substances, and self.*
LLOYD D. NEWELL[24]

I was speaking on a program once with Emma Lou Thayne. She is a wise and gifted writer. On this particular day, she shared with a group of seminary students a tender and personal story of her daughter's battle with an eating disorder. She openly discussed her own struggle as a mother, trying to help her daughter. It was touching. Afterwards I said to Emma Lou, "I am in awe of your willingness to be so personal about your own difficulties. I don't know that I could do that."

I will never forget her answer. She turned to look at me

squarely, but with understanding. Her gentle response went something like this: "Virginia, our stories are what make the difference, and if we can tell them honestly we can hope to help each other. In the end, we have nothing to offer each other but our stories."

When I open-heartedly offer my stories to you, both of us feel less alone. We both feel braver, stronger, and more completely loved.

Take a look at your own comfort with reciprocity. Be honest as you think about yourself.

We've all listened to personal stories, gifts given to us by others; stories that stay with us forever, continuing to feed and teach and inspire us. We hear them in Relief Society, at the playground while we watch the children swing, and over lunch. Jot down one or two of those that have stuck in your mind over the years. If possible, thank the person who told you her story. Tell her how important it has been to you—how long you have remembered it and why.

What about your stories? Take a risk by writing or telling an experience you had when you felt vulnerable or alone. Share it with someone who might benefit from it.

# Chapter Six

# REPORTING

———— ❧ ————

*Soft, morning air*

*Visible to secret keepers*

*Tucking conversation into a quiet canyon*

*A corner where it's safe*

*Until tomorrow,*

*Or weeks or months from now.*

*Real life and wandering words*

*Slowly expose*

*Precisely chiseled*

*Truth.*

—V. PEARCE

Experience is the raw material of life. It is abundantly available to every person. We can use it to discover, grow, and change; or we can simply let it happen and keep breathing until something else happens, never using what we have learned to positively influence and shape future experiences.

Therapists sometimes use a technique called "framing" to empower clients in their own lives. With this technique, a person examines the experience and with the therapist discovers what happened, why it happened, and then defines ways to consciously repeat the experience if it is a positive one, or to avoid repeating the experience if it is negative. Framing is an efficient way to avoid making the same mistakes over and over, or conversely, to ensure repeating actions that produce good results. It is a way to take charge and learn from the raw material of life.

When I wish to accelerate personal change I find it critical to have someone who will help me to do some "framing." This is undoubtedly the trickiest part of the Christianity 101 experiment. While it takes no extra time or planning to simply be

———— ❧ ————

*Meditation is the language of the soul. . . . Meditation is one of the most secret, most sacred doors through which we pass into the presence of the Lord. . . . To have communion with God, through his Holy Spirit, is one of the noblest aspirations of life. It is when the peace of love of God have entered the soul, when serving him becomes the motivating factor in one's life and existence.*

PRESIDENT DAVID O. MCKAY[25]

more aware of the condition of your heart and then to change it, it will take a bit of planning to find someone who can help you figure out what is going on.

Find someone who is just as interested as you are in experimenting. It may be the friend you walk or exercise with. It may be book club friends or coworkers. It may be a spouse, an adult child, or one of your siblings. It may be a visiting teaching partner or someone you visit teach. It may be a neighbor or cousin. If the person or people you find choose not to experiment themselves, ask if they would be willing to talk with you about your own experiences.

*Therefore, strengthen your brethren in all your conversation, in all your prayers, in all your exhortations, and in all your doings.*
D&C 108:7

Set a specific time to report. Shorter intervals between reporting times will help you develop new attitudes more quickly. One week is a good amount of time, but if you are walking every day with someone, it's easy to report more often. If you have to set up a special meeting time, you may only be able to meet once a month. If you can't find someone to debrief with, write. Composing letters or journal entries will help you figure things out.

Be honest. The outcome of an experiment by definition is not predictable. This isn't a test. An experiment is simply a way to learn. Your actions, feelings, and observations will necessarily be different than anyone else's. If you are honest in reporting, then you will be able to learn something that has value for you.

> *We took sweet counsel together, and walked unto the house of God in company.*
> PSALM 55:14

Identify personal red flags. I am convinced that each of us has stumbling blocks peculiar to ourselves. Remember Ellen who baked the cinnamon rolls? Doing so helped her to overcome her shyness. She discovered an important red flag for her: when she felt her habitual shyness creeping on, it meant that her heart was closing. She simply had to talk back to the shyness if she wanted to increase her ability to feel and give God's love. Pauline was fearful that she would look stupid when she couldn't remember her friend's name at the gym. She saw that as a pattern. Her easily recognized red flag was that flight from someone when you are pretending to know something you don't know—a very common manifestation of pride. I was repeatedly concerned that cultivating an open heart would require too much extra time. When I feel that way now, I recognize it as a gate locked against my heart. I can then respond more appropriately. These problems and many more became irrelevant as we experimented. We found that shyness is not terminal, that in fact, people don't think you are stupid if you forget their names, and that time is not the issue we sometimes think it is. Discover what your reflexive thoughts are—the ones that keep your heart locked up tight. When you find out what they are, then you can evaluate whether they are rational or not and whether you should experiment with changing them.

Pay attention to spiritual confirmations. Is the Spirit working in this? Do you feel confirmations of comfort, peace, and happiness? Are the seeds beginning to swell?

> *And when you feel these swelling motions, ye will begin to say within yourselves—It must needs be that this is a good seed, or that the word is good, for it beginneth to enlarge my soul; yea, it beginneth to enlighten my understanding, yea, it beginneth to be delicious to me.*
>
> ALMA 32:28

When I began this experiment with my Relief Society committee, we were meeting about once a month already so that is what we chose to continue doing. The first month brought few results; perhaps because we were such amateurs and there was too much forgetting time. However, after our first sharing time, the excitement increased and our experiences increased, probably because the meeting and talking increased our awareness and our anticipation of possible results. Within a couple of months we had established some new habits and developed a testimony of the principles that we then planned to teach at our stake women's conference.

The "Hawthorne Effect" is a term used to describe the tendency of subjects in experiments to increase sought-after behavior or decrease negative behavior, simply because they are being studied. It was first observed among the employees at the Hawthorne Plant who were being studied by researchers from Harvard Business School. The researchers were studying worker productivity. But they encountered a problem. When the researchers gave attention to the employees, the workers' productivity didn't remain static, it increased. This change in productivity was produced simply by an awareness that they were being studied, and it skewed the study.

> *I'm going to make a suggestion to each of you. On the next fast day, take occasion and arrange your affairs in such a way that you can be by yourself, maybe under a tree in the backyard, maybe in the locked bedroom of your home, where you can think. Read the scriptures and think of sacred things and think of yourself.*
>
> PRESIDENT GORDON B. HINCKLEY[26]

Obviously, the Hawthorne Effect drives researchers crazy, but for those who wish to change behavior it is quite encouraging. It means that all I have to do to increase the frequency of a desired behavior, or decrease the frequency of a negative behavior, is to notice it! Just my awareness of it will change the results. Is that slick? I think so.

For instance, if a mother is concerned about how often she speaks in habitually negative language to her children, she can decide to count all of the negative statements she makes. Without any apparent self-discipline, as she becomes aware of how many times a day she responds to a child negatively, she will instinctively improve. Being aware enough to count and report our experiences is a dynamic and positive process.

> *Brethren, we need to meditate more. We're so busy doing little things. We need to meditate more.*
> PRESIDENT DAVID O. MCKAY[27]

If you can't find anyone to report to and writing is not practical, at the very least, count and record. You could fill one pocket with pennies at the beginning of the day, and each time you feel your heart expanding, opening, and reaching out to another person, take one penny and transfer it to the other pocket. At the end of the day, write down the number of pennies in the second pocket. I have done this to self-monitor all sorts of behaviors, and the Hawthorne Effect always holds true. As I continue to count and record, the positive behaviors increase and the negative behaviors decrease. Quite easy.

> *The life which is unexamined is not worth living.*
> PLATO[28]

Along with reporting and counting, pondering over this experiment in Christianity can be productive. Taking time alone to think and pray is all too rare in a busy and fast-moving world. It just doesn't happen if it isn't consciously programmed into life. Fast Sundays, now that my children are grown and gone, usually give me a few minutes of extra time with my scriptures and my thoughts. When our home was full of children, there seemed to be no time for meditating on Sundays, fast Sunday or otherwise. But I found that on Mondays, if I were vigilant, I could find a way to have my own quiet time for reflection and renewal.

No matter your choice of person, place, or time to do your reporting, just make sure you do it. It is very often in the act of reporting that the Holy Ghost chooses to witness and confirm the actions. And ultimately, it is the confirmation of the Spirit that provides the best motivation to keep doing good things.

# Chapter Seven

# A New Heart

꧁❦꧂

*A new heart also will I give you,*
*and a new spirit will I put within you:*
*and I will take away the stony heart out of your flesh,*
*and I will give you an heart of flesh.*

Ezekiel 36:26

My friend Barbara and I went to a funeral recently. It was a beautiful autumn day, and the somberness of death created a quiet space. On the way home our mood of reflection matched the gathering clouds over our tree-lined neighborhood. We talked about the precious nature of friendship and our belief in eternal ties. The conversation wove its way back to our discovery of Christianity 101 several years before—how exciting it was for us and what fun we had. We remembered how we had laughed when Barbara asked if it counted if she opened her heart to someone on the plane, not someone in our stake! During the few months after that first meeting, she had shared a half dozen more encounters, all of them meaningful. I wondered if she felt permanently changed the way I do.

"Do you think about our grand experiment every once in a while? I mean, does it still work for you?" I asked as I steered my car into her driveway and slowed down so I wouldn't scrape the bottom of the car coming out of the gutter and onto the driveway—again.

She shook that wonderful blonde hair out of her face as she chuckled, "I'll say it works. And I keep discovering new and wonderful things about it."

"Really?" I said, wanting to help her keep talking.

"Yes. I feel so much freer," Barbara continued, taking her hand off the door handle and turning toward me. "I guess one of the things that I didn't know before our experiment was that when you honestly open your heart up to someone it is a gift. And if they don't take the gift, it's still okay because I did my part, and I still win because I feel so good. Remember how much we talked about this being a change inside *us,* regardless of any other change?"

"Yes, I think I know what you mean. Are you in a hurry? We could talk about this some other time," I said. Reaching for the shift stick, I prepared to put the car in reverse. There I was again, always worried about time! When will I ever learn!

"Oh, no. It's great to have someone to talk to again. I miss being able to talk about it with all of you," Barbara said. I turned the ignition off and repositioned myself toward her.

"Then go ahead. You know that *I'm* the time freak. I'm still trying to get over that!"

"Well, I feel so much better myself." She looked toward the kids walking down the street, on their way home from school. "In the beginning, I thought that I was opening my heart so that the other person would for sure feel how much the Lord loved them and they would change. You know, their hearts would soften and open? I guess I've always been conditionally kind. When people responded, great. When they didn't, I pulled right back—back

———— ❧ ————

*It is a very small matter* to you *whether the man give you your right or not: it is life or death to you whether or not you give him his. Whether he pay you what you count his debt or no, you will be compelled to pay him all you owe him. If you owe him a pound and he you a million, you must pay him the pound whether he pay you the million or not; there is no business parallel here. If, owing you love, he gives you hate, you, owing him love, have yet to pay it.*
GEORGE MACDONALD[29]

to a hardened little heart with a protective wall around it. But I'm changing." She twisted around in her seat to face me again, tucking one foot up on the seat underneath herself.

"I mean, let me tell you about a woman I visit teach," she said, leaning forward as if this were a delightfully forbidden conspiracy. "She left the Church a long time ago—at least, she has never been active in our ward. She's never seemed to want any contact with me. She would come to the door and say a few things or we'd have brief talks on the telephone, but it was pretty guarded. Then I remembered our experiment, and I began to pray before contacting her. I prayed about my heart, and I tried to be aware of it. I wanted the Lord to help me open my heart, to fill me with His love so that it would overflow to her. I prayed to see her as the Lord sees her. And honestly, Virginia, it was that easy. Everything started to change."

Barbara threw back her head and laughed, "Funniest thing. One day my daughter and I were in the car running errands. It was near the end of the month, and I hadn't contacted my friend yet. I said, 'Just wait in the car while I run this visiting teaching message to the door. Don't worry. I'll only be a minute, because she never lets me in.' Well, of course, that was the day. Not only did she invite me in, but she wanted to tell me all about herself. She told me why she didn't come to church anymore—what had happened. While I let her talk, I noticed that my heart was right on the surface, honoring this wonderful woman. We ended up crying together, hugging, and I went back to the car to face an irate teenager! You can imagine how mad she was. 'I thought you said you weren't even going in!' It was hard for me to be very convincing when I said I was sorry, because I was ecstatic about what had just happened."

Barbara repositioned herself again, taking her foot out from under her and tucking her hair behind one ear. I turned on the key and opened her window, then mine. It was getting hot. "But the part I wanted to tell you about was that when I called the next month she was quite standoffish. And it's been kind of off and on still. Just the other day, she said to me on the telephone, 'I think I've told you too much and I just can't have you visit for a while.' I might have felt rejected in the past, but now that I'm aware that *my* heart and its condition is the thing I have control over—not hers—it's not a problem. And the fact that she can talk about what she needs or doesn't need, really says that her heart is open after all.

"Regardless of what she does or doesn't do, I like living with an open heart. And I'm going to do whatever it takes to keep it that way!"

"I know what you mean," I said, leaning forward. "I used

to do that too. The least little rejection and it was all over. I had a friend once who agreed to hear the missionaries. When she didn't respond and get baptized I couldn't seem to just be a friend again. I felt so rejected. Until we learned about opening our hearts to others I didn't understand what had happened. Now those missionary opportunities are just part of the free-flowing back and forth, and I find it easy to continue loving and caring when someone chooses not to believe because I really care about them as unique and loveable individuals, not just potential baptisms."

Now we were almost fighting for our talking time, inter-rupting with excitement, nodding in agreement.

Barbara started again, "I know what you mean, because the other ah-ha for me is that it's not just about getting my friend back to church either. I guess I always thought that was my job when I was given someone to visit teach who wasn't active. I've changed my mind. I think my job, if you could call it a job, is more about helping her feel for herself how much she is loved by me—and more than that, how much she is loved by the Lord. When she feels that, really feels it, the things that she needs will come along at the pace that's right for her. I trust that so much more."

Barbara's son poked his head in the window. "Hey, you

guys. I need to back my car out. Could you move the car to the side of the driveway?"

We both laughed. "I've got to go, anyway," I said as Barbara reached for the door handle, hopped out, and turned around to wave. "Thanks for the jabber-time," she laughed.

Another year passed. Once again, that thing September always does to me—just a little slowing down time to remember—an awareness that life is moving on and a desire to look back just for a minute. It's that song from *The Fantastiks*, "Try to remember a time in September . . . then follow . . . follow . . . follow . . ."

"I need some get-together time. How about any or all of you? Lunch? A hike? Just talking? I especially want to know where you all are with the Open Heart thing. Have you forgotten all about it or does it still work? Hit the reply button and let me know when would be a good time," I wrote in a group e-mail to some of my experimenting friends of bygone days.

So there we were yesterday afternoon in a circle again, catching up, chattering like magpies on a clothesline: newly engaged children, new in-laws, new babies, new teenagers, new church callings, new jobs.

Just for a moment I closed my own mouth and sat back on the sofa to listen. I felt old, as if I could see the unrelenting parade of life—day after day, year after year, always adapting, wondering if there's a better way to figure it all out and do it right or if we just stumble along—like guerilla warfare, where you are constantly ambushed and you keep fighting, but take no permanent ground.

"What about the open heart stuff," I asked, elbowing myself back into the conversation, "is it gone or does it still seem relevant?" The next hour was eerily reminiscent of our first meeting those many years before.

"I'm just so busy."

"I'm not in a Relief Society calling anymore and I've sort of lost permission to be in other people's lives in the same way."

"Life just keeps moving and you forget." Then slowly the momentum changed.

"Actually, I was the recipient of an open heart this summer. And I thought of it that way at the time," Pauline said. "It was at Rough Out Camp. I'm new in Young Women and feel pretty inept. I especially felt like I was on the edge of everything the first day of camp. But after I had done my little bit on a fire-side program, one of the girls told me (with a hug) that what I had said mattered to her. There is no way she will ever know how important her open-hearted hug was to me! It reminded me . . . again.

"So, I want to be better, but I *can* say that there are a few permanent changes. I never, *absolutely never,* walk into Sunday School and sit by myself on the back row like I always used to. And I say hello to people, even if I'm not completely sure who they are or if they know me." Pauline giggled and looked at me. "I mean, a couple of weeks ago I saw your husband out walking, Virginia, and I waved and said, 'Hello, Jim.' It's stupid, but I'm surprised at how often I *don't* automatically do that sort of thing and then have to remind myself that no one is likely to be offended if you remember them and call out a greeting. And it might make them feel good. Why would I hold back just because I don't know someone very well?!"

Wendy, thoughtfully attentive as always, slowly started. "Maybe this is a quirky way to look at it, but I'm seeing changes in teachers in my Relief Society who accept and encourage people in the class to share their experiences. And our Relief Society leaders are listening and watching everyone and responding to what their needs are. In our ward, we have several midweek activities going on: young mothers and children taking field trips, walking groups, family history groups, a weekly young mother education class, midday luncheons for widows, book groups. I think that they are an evidence of respecting and acknowledging individual needs. We really have an open-hearted Relief Society presidency.

"I was teaching the Gospel Doctrine class a few weeks ago when my husband made a comment that seemed irrelevant to the current lesson. The material he referred to had been previously covered, and I felt a review would have been a distraction. He said something like, 'Aren't you going to talk about the organization of the Relief Society in Nauvoo?' I said, 'No, we talked about it last week,' rather snippy and moved on.

"As I continued the lesson I thought, *That was a shriveled heart kind of thing to say.* Not only was an apology in order to my husband but to the class. In my closing remarks, I said, 'I'm sorry for the way I handled my husband's question about the Relief Society organization. I apologize to him and to you. I'm sorry.' This was one of my better teaching moments . . . a real situation of repentance. And my heart immediately felt different.

"Can I tell one more story? I know everyone needs a chance to talk, but it was so great."

She was already talking as we murmured assent. "One of the teachers in our Relief Society shared a time in her life when she faced a 'brick wall.' She didn't know where to turn for help. Prior to a court hearing, she had tried everything she could think of as a single mother to help the professionals involved with her children to understand her situation. She felt they were asking questions that did not give the true picture of what was happening to the children when they were with their father. She felt alone and misunderstood. 'Where was God when she needed Him?' She prayed again and again. No answers. However, as the hearing progressed the judge did understand and made a helpful judgment for her and the children. As we in the class listened, we thought of times in our lives when we, too, felt unheard. We identified with the teacher and loved and appreciated her. We had in front of us an example of patience and faith. It's that kind of open-hearted teaching that makes a real difference to us all, I think."

"Speaking of Relief Society, I was given a new visiting teaching assignment that included a very difficult woman," Ellen chimed in "When I went to visit her the first time, I remembered your stories, the experiences you all shared during our committee meetings. I realized that I had to watch my heart because it would be easy to be critical and keep a wall between us. When I listen to her it's helpful to pay less attention to her words and more attention to her feelings. Uh-huh, I think there are permanent changes in me, because I seem to keep drawing on your stories when I get in a difficult spot."

"Did anyone talk to Susan?" someone asked.

"Yes, she sent me a fun e-mail. She wanted to be here, but they're out of town. Let me read it to you. 'Dear Virginia, I can't tell you what a wonderful time I just had experimenting again with an "open heart" at the U.S. Open Tennis Tournament! I talked with women from all over the world, and even a few men. I even talked in Spanish with women from Venezuela and a couple from Mexico City. It was so fun. I think I have become more willing to take a chance and not worry about seeming too forward or intrusive. Everyone I talked to seemed to enjoy sharing about themselves and learning about me.

"'I wish I could come although I'm not sure how much I can remember or contribute. I would love to hear what others have to say. Love, Susan.'"

Pauline shifted in her seat and asked, "Does anybody else think it's pretty easy to be more open with strangers—people you don't see all the time, rather than your close friends or family? I'm still pretty bad at home."

"Yeah," we all nodded. "I wonder why?"

The question hung in the air for a moment, each of us turning it over.

"Maybe it's the busyness. There's so much to get done."

"Right. Just think of it, Pauline. You've had two weddings this year, one next week, and another daughter on the verge. That's a lot of stuff to do!"

"It might be more than just busyness," Barbara said rather tentatively. "We had the most amazing experience this summer. We went to Bolivia on a humanitarian service project. We worked so hard and when it was over we had a church meeting. They asked me to speak. It was so tender because my returned missionary son translated. I felt so much coming from the audience to me and so much coming from above. I was transported and was literally filled with spiritual power. Afterwards, everyone hugged and kissed me. It was really something. I was truly beyond myself—a person I had never been before. Then I found myself in my own ward the next Sunday, just a little person again. It was confusing. I hadn't thought about it until now, but maybe I was able to experience a huge opening of heart because the people in Brazil expected so much—they just opened their hearts to me, thinking that because I was from Salt Lake I would feed them spiritually. I responded by opening my heart, and the Lord literally filled all of us with His love. It was amazing."

"So," I said, knowing that Pauline was on a tight schedule and needed to get home, "we all keep having experiences, but do you think in these past few years there has been any *permanent* change? Are we changed inside enough that we automatically *do* things differently?"

"I would have said 'no,' when we first started talking today," Ellen responded, "but after sitting here, I've changed my mind. Look how we all know how to think about and talk about what happens. I think that's an amazing change. And aren't all of us saying that we're habitually more comfortable talking to people we wouldn't otherwise talk to? That makes me think that we are becoming different."

"Yeah, you're right," Barbara chimed in. "I guess what I'm interested in now is the challenge to be more open-hearted toward people I know well—my family especially. Whatever the reason, I think that's a more difficult thing for all of us. Ah-ha," she laughed, "Experiment, Part B!"

"I'm willing to try anything if we can get together again. How about lunch in a few months—maybe after the Christmas holidays?" I asked.

The scriptures call it a "new heart." When Samuel anointed Saul to be king and prophet we are told that "God gave him another heart" (1 Samuel 10:9). Paul taught that "if any man be in Christ, he is a new creature" (2 Corinthians 5:17).

In the definition of *Conversion,* the Bible Dictionary says that conversion "denotes changing one's views, in a conscious acceptance of the will of God (Acts 3:19). If followed by continued faith in the Lord Jesus Christ, repentance, baptism in water for the remission of sins, and the reception of the Holy Ghost by the laying on of hands, conversion will become complete, and will change a natural man into a sanctified, born again, purified person—a new creature in Christ Jesus (see 2 Cor. 5:17)."

We are each spiritually begotten sons and daughters of God, but Heavenly Father tells us that we become His sons and daughters in a different and more profound way when we become true followers of his Son, Jesus Christ.

Perhaps this is the "new man" that C. S. Lewis describes: "Every now and then one meets them. Their very voices and faces are different from ours: stronger, quieter, happier, more radiant. They begin where most of us leave off. They are, I say, recognisable; but you must know what to look for. . . . They do not draw attention to themselves. . . . They love you more than other men do, but they need you less. (We must get over wanting to be needed: in some goodish people, specially women, that is the hardest of all temptations to resist.) They will usually seem to have a lot of time; you will wonder where it comes from." Lewis says that this new way of being is something we get from Christ. "He transmits it not by heredity but by what I have called 'good infection.' Everyone who gets it gets it by personal contact with Him. Other men become 'new' by being 'in Him.'"[30]

Do you see why it is vital to be filled with His love? It doesn't just make life nicer or more pleasant and comfortable. Being filled with the love of God actually changes everything because it has the power to completely change us inside. You see, over time, it changes us from the natural man into a true son or daughter of God, a sanctified being—one who has finally become like Him. And that's what we're here on earth to do—to become like Him and help others do the same.

I want a heart like His. What about you?

# SOURCES

1. Bonnie D. Parkin, in "Feeling the Love of the Lord Daily in Our Lives," *Ensign*, January 2004, 67.

2. Dallin H. Oaks, "The Challenge to Become," *Ensign*, November 2000, 32, 33, 34.

3. Marilyn Arnold, "The Turning of Hearts in the Book of Mormon," in Susette Fletcher Green, Dawn Hall Anderson, and Dlora Hall Dalton, eds., *Hearts Knit Together: Talks from the 1995 Women's Conference* (Salt Lake City: Deseret Book, 1996), 184.

4. Dr. Seuss, *How the Grinch Stole Christmas* (New York: Random House, 1957), 50.

5. Joseph Smith, *History of The Church of Jesus Christ of Latter-day Saints,* ed. B. H. Roberts, 2d ed. rev., 7 vols. (Salt Lake City: The Church of Jesus Christ of Latter-day Saints, 1932–51), 4:606.

6. Gordon B. Hinckley, *Discourses of President Gordon B. Hinckley, vol. 1: 1995–1999* (Salt Lake City: Deseret Book, 2005), 310.

7. C. Terry Warner, *Bonds That Make Us Free* (Salt Lake City: Shadow Mountain, 2001), 46.

8. John H. Groberg, "The Power of God's Love," *Ensign*, November 2004, 11.

9. John H. Groberg, "The Power of God's Love," *Ensign,* November 2004, 9.

10. "Each Life That Touches Ours for Good," *Hymns of The Church of Jesus Christ of Latter-day Saints* (Salt Lake City: The Church of Jesus Christ of Latter-day Saints, 1985), no. 293.

11. James E. Faust, "The Atonement: Our Greatest Hope," *Ensign,* November 2001, 20.

12. John A. Widtsoe, "The Worth of Souls," *Utah Genealogical and Historical Magazine* 25 (October 1934): 189–90.

13. John Taylor, in *Journal of Discourses,* 26 vols. (London: Latter-day Saints' Book Depot, 1854–86), 17:176.

14. Martin Luther, quoted in Lewis Spitz, *The Renaissance and Reformation Movements* (Chicago: Rand McNally, 1971), 335.

15. C. S. Lewis, *Mere Christianity* (New York: HarperCollins, 2001), 226.

16. *Glimpses into the Life and Heart of Marjorie Pay Hinckley,* edited by Virigina H. Pearce (Salt Lake City: Deseret Book, 1999), 175–76.

17. Mary Lou Kownacki, "For Rose, an Untouchable," in *Between Two Souls: Conversations with Ryokan* (Grand Rapids, Mich.: Wm. B. Eerdmans Publishing Co., 2004), 123.

18. Boyd K. Packer, *Teach Ye Diligently* (Salt Lake City: Deseret Book, 2005), 94–95.

19. Albert Schweitzer, *Memoirs of Childhood and Youth* (New York: Macmillan, 1950), 77–78.

20. Neal A. Maxwell, "Jesus, the Perfect Mentor," *Ensign,* February 2001, 8.

21. Mother Teresa, in Malcolm Muggeridge, *Something*

*Beautiful for God: Mother Teresa of Calcutta* (New York: Walker and Company/Phoenix Press, 1971; large print edition 1984), 64.

22. Evelyn P. Henriksen, quoted in *Glimpses into the Life and Heart of Marjorie Pay Hinckley,* edited by Virigina H. Pearce (Salt Lake City: Deseret Book, 1999), 37–38.

23. John Steinbeck, "In Awe of Words," in *The Exonian,* 75th anniversary edition (Exeter University; repr. in *Writers at Work,* Fourth Series, ed. by George Plimpton, 1977).

24. Lloyd D. Newell, *May Peace Be with You* (Salt Lake City: Deseret Book, 1994), 135.

25. David O. McKay, in Conference Report, April 1967, 85, 133.

26. Gordon B. Hinckley, *Teachings of Gordon B. Hinckley* (Salt Lake City: Deseret Book, 1997), 335.

27. David O. McKay, quoted in Gordon B. Hinckley, *Teachings of Gordon B. Hinckley* (Salt Lake City: Deseret Book, 1997), 334.

28. Plato, *Apology 38 Thesaurus,* 93a.

29. *George MacDonald Anthology,* edited by C. S. Lewis (New York: HarperCollins, 2001), 60–61.

30. C. S. Lewis, *Mere Christianity* (New York: HarperCollins, 2001), 223, 221.

# INDEX

———— ❧ ————